A Change of Presence

David Adelberg

PUBLISH AMERICA

PublishAmerica
Baltimore

First printing

ISBN: 1-4137-6159-3
PUBLISHED BY PUBLISHAMERICA, LLLP
www.publishamerica.com
Baltimore

Printed in the United States of America

Acknowledgments

Patty Malone... Your words of encouragement gave me back my life.

Bill Gilmore... Thank you. I couldn't have done it without you.

Prologue

I found it between the folds of an old pink blanket in a chocolate box in my grandmother's cedar chest. It was in remarkable shape considering it was taken in the spring of 1919.

He wore a wide-brimmed canvas hat with a chinstrap, a whitish shirt, and two vests, one buttoned and one made of leather that hung open over the other. I couldn't tell whether or not he had hair. I assumed he didn't. My father has been bald since he was twenty. He was standing in front of a six-foot fence, holding a rifle. A black bear cub stood precariously on the fence post behind him and rested a paw on his shoulder.

My grandfather died in the fall of 1926; he was seventy-six years old. I started to do the math. He was born in 1850; that's a hundred and fifty-four years ago. Somehow it didn't make sense. Somewhere I had lost a generation. I thought about how things might have been different if only I had been able to talk to him just once. Maybe he would have opened up to me and told me about all those years before he met my grandmother. He was already over fifty when he and Bubba married, and she was still a young woman when he died. My aunt told me it was quite common back then; love was rarely a consideration. Young men were hard to find; it mattered little how old they were. It was difficult just to find a husband never mind one that could protect them and provide a roof over their heads.

I focused on his face. I think he was smiling but I couldn't be sure. I wondered who had taken the picture. I couldn't imagine how a photographer ended up in one of the most remote places in the world just to take a picture of my grandfather.

Chapter One

It took almost three years and five hundred thousand British troops to force the Dutch to capitulate; when they did, it was more like a few gentleman friends just sitting around the fire smoking cigars and drinking brandy, talking bipartisan politics, rather than surrender. There was already a hundred and fifty thousand dead, mostly civilians.

Diamonds; a land saturated with them. The Rothschilds, undoubtedly the world's smartest businessmen, decided to loan the Empire the money to fight the Dutch in exchange for the diamonds. But in the end, Her Majesty, although grateful for their help, declared it wasn't appropriate for anyone, let alone Jews, to be seen as having bought a country. So, the Empire would pay off the "war loan" by selling the diamonds back to the Rothschilds at a price set by the Rothschilds. In other words, for the next fifty years the wealthiest family in the world would pay nothing for the diamonds.

The Rothschilds needed the British Empire's military might to destroy the Dutch and simply take the mines from them. Her Majesty appointed Cecil Rhodes as her representative, and he and he alone would negotiate the terms of surrender. He and he alone would insure the Rothschilds ended up with the diamonds.

Though the war was over, it would be two more years before the rebels were finally crushed. Many in England couldn't understand why the rebels continued to fight knowing there was no hope, but like every occupation in history, the conquered were driven to avenge their fallen comrades and take back what was stolen from them. Mostly farmers and sheep herders, the rebels fought unlike any army the British had ever encountered before. This ragged group of warriors showed no mercy and struck without warning, finding new and innovative ways to kill. The British newspapers called them terrorists and guerrillas, hence the term now known as guerrilla warfare.

Among the wealthiest early mine owners was Randolph Kimberly. During the war he had found a way not only to stay neutral but made a deal with Paul Kruger, the president of the Dutch colony, to allow him to continue operating the mines even while the British army lay at their doorstep. When Kruger surrendered, the flow of diamonds to Europe suddenly increased a thousand percent, and a time of unprecedented prosperity unfolded for the British and even more so for those Dutch and English businessmen who had forsaken the Boer settlers in exchange for economic and personal gains.

Lord Kimberly loathed tardiness; God help any of the office people if they showed up late. His Lordship made a habit of humiliating employees. He hated them; they were Jews, and if not for his contractual obligations, he would have thrown them out long ago.

At seventy-two he still ruled Kimberly Mines like a man possessed. He waited in his office until the stroke of eight, opened the double doors and slowly marched down the center aisle of the outer office that separated the worktables. The diamond handlers stood by their stations with their palms up while His Lordship satisfied himself that nothing was amiss. Every tool had to be placed exactly where it had to be. If it wasn't, there would be hell to pay.

His usual frown deepened as he reached the end. Without a single infraction, Lord Kimberly had no choice but to keep walking; his day at the office was over. He walked through the open outer office doors and yelled for his servant.

"Franks!"

"Coming, sir!"

Douglas Franks suspected they were stealing; he longed for the day when he could rip the clothes of those Jewish bastards. With pocketless suits, they would have to put them up their asses or down their throats; if they did, he'd tear the diamonds out of them.

Clouds of blue smoke fell over the brass desk candles, becoming fluorescent as they passed through the narrow rays of light that crisscrossed the dark walls of the library.

"She's late again, my lord."

"Ah, yes, Franks, what would you do? Never mind; what would you know about raising a child?"

"A child, My Lord? I believe Miss Dina is past the child stage."

"That will be enough, Franks! My granddaughter's stages are not your concern."

"Of course, My Lord. I would simply remind you of Miss Dina's eighteenth birthday."

"I'm well aware, Franks. I assure you, there won't be a problem."

"I'm sure you're right, My Lord; I only wish I shared your optimism."

"Why do you go on about this, Franks? For God's sake, she's my granddaughter; she'll do exactly what I tell her to do."

"Perhaps you haven't noticed, My Lord, but Miss Dina stopped doing what she was told a long time ago."

Lord Kimberly would have hardly noticed; one Sunday afternoon a week was all the time he ever spent with his intelligent granddaughter.

After three years in an English finishing school, Dina Kimberly returned to Johannesburg minus her propensity for overeating. Although she found her school chums entertaining, she never considered remaining there. When reports that war between the Dutch and German settlers and England was inevitable, Dina felt compelled to be right in the middle of it. She had been fascinated with and majored in English military history, a class that wasn't offered to women, but with being heir to the Kimberly fortune, she had no difficulty in getting it included in her course curriculum. In fact, Dina never had difficulty in getting anything she wanted. Now equipped with a perfect figure, dark blonde hair and beautiful green eyes, Dina's desires were never refused by anyone. The only person that ever said no to her was Tawney. She had been her mother's nanny, and would be her daughter's if she ever had a daughter. Looking at herself in the floor length mirror, she wondered if there would ever be a man in her life, a man who would challenge her, a man who would stand up to her grandfather and not be intimidated by the repulsive Mister Franks.

"Honestly, Dina, you've been standing in front of that mirror for an hour; have you no shame?" Dina tilted her head and raised her hip to her hand.

"I can't help it," she said. "I keep thinking I'll be old and gray before anyone else sees me like this."

"If someone sees you in that getup, you'll need an army to keep them off."

"What do you think Grandfather would say if he saw me like this?"

"I can't imagine."

"Now, Tawney, surely Grandfather must have seen a woman in her underwear once upon a time."

"If he did, she didn't look like you; and I'm sure it was so long ago he's forgotten about it anyway. Now please, Dina, get into this dress; you know how your grandfather will go on if you're late."

"I guess I'm ready, Tawney. Is there anyone else joining us? I hope someone shows up; I can only take so much of Grandfather dominating the conversation. Besides, he has no idea of what is really happening in our country, and I get bored trying to explain it to him."

"Now, Dina, I'm not sure all that schooling was a good thing. Your mother was well-educated, but she never found it necessary to embarrass those who were less informed."

"You're just saying that; my mother was a hellcat. She didn't hesitate to follow my father into battle without Grandfather's blessing. She was destined to rule this country, and if not for a freak hurricane, she would, I'm sure, still be running it."

Tawney readjusted the position of Dina's hairpin, held her shoulders and gently turned her around and looked fondly into her eyes.

"Your mother was foolish; I tried to stop her but she wouldn't listen, and now her daughter wants to break my heart."

"No one will break your heart," she said, as she wiped a tear from the corner of Tawney's black cheek. "What would I do without you? You are my only friend; I will never let anyone break your heart."

Dina could feel Tawney's tears on her neck as she embraced her.

"What is it, Tawney? Why do you weep so?"

"You will break my heart if you send me away," she said.

"Why on earth would I send you away? Now stop, my darling; tell me what's troubling you."

Dina led her lifelong friend to the edge of her bed and sat next to her.

"Your father didn't die in a hurricane, Dina," she said.

"What are you saying, Tawney? Of course he did."

"No! Your grandfather found out he was Jewish and threw him in prison the same day your mother fell to her death. I'm so sorry, Dina. Your grandfather made me swear not to tell you. If he knew I had, he'd have me killed! Please, Dina, please don't tell him."

"Where is my father?" Dina demanded. "Is he still in prison? How can I find him?"

"I don't know, Dina. Your father was a resourceful man; only weeks after he was jailed he escaped. No one has heard from him since. It may have been a rumor but it was thought he must have joined up with the Dutch rebels but..."

"Never mind that now, Tawney, just start packing."

From thirty feet above the marble entrance, Dina began her descent down the dark mahogany staircase of the Kimberly mansion. Douglas Franks stopped on his way to answering the door chimes and watched her from the bottom of the stairs. She sensed his stare but, as usual, refused to acknowledge it. Her grandfather's valet, or bodyguard, or whatever he was, had always been sickly respectful to her, but there was something about him, something that made her terribly uncomfortable.

Franks stood motionless, mesmerized by her beauty. He wanted to touch her as she passed in front of him, but the urge was quickly replaced with repulsion and hatred, hatred for her father and repulsion by the stench of Jewish blood.

Her grandfather's library was a man's room, one of the few that Dina even considered spending more than a second in. She disliked frills and unnecessary lace. The tightly tailored striped forest green dress was of her own design; it accentuated her long neck and straight shoulders as well as her ample breasts.

"Good afternoon, Grandfather," she said. "What's the news from England?"

Dina poured herself a cup of tea and sat on the upholstered chair across from her grandfather.

"I expect ten thousand to rid me of those who would destroy what I have built." It was more a mumble than an attempt to communicate.

"I wonder what kind of reception they will receive," she said. "Another ten thousand might be just the fuse you've been looking for, don't you think, Grandfather?"

"I wish you spent your time with more womanly things, Dina; politics is not your concern."

"My concerns are the concerns of millions; military supremacy will not change the inevitable, Grandfather."

"You sound more like your mother every day," he said.

"I'll take that as a compliment, Grandfather. I imagine she caused you as much distress."

"Lord Smyth, My Lord." Frank's sudden interruption caused a slight tremor to Dina's cup and saucer.

"Ah yes, Smyth, come, my good man; allow me to introduce my granddaughter."

He was tall, almost awkward as he approached her. He placed his grey top hat under his arm and bowed with all the grace that only the finest of educations could provide.

"A sublime pleasure, Miss Kimberly," he said.

"Lord Smyth, I was hoping for company; please sit. Tea?"

She loved the game; an English finishing school did that to you. Her friends were excellent teachers; they prided themselves on having trained the very beautiful and naive girl from the colony.

"Lord Smyth has some papers for you to sign, my dear. Perhaps we should get this out of the way before we get too comfortable. You have them, Smyth?"

"Yes, My Lord." The handsome young solicitor removed a series of documents from a leather case and spread them out on the marble topped table before her. Lord Kimberly provided the quill and ink.

"Please sign where Smyth shows you, Dina."

Her bewilderment quickly passed as she took the pen from her grandfather and slowly placed it back on the table.

"What are these about, Grandfather? I've not had to sign documents before; why is this necessary?"

"This is extremely important, Dina; now just sign them! You do not need to know their intent."

"I'm sorry, Grandfather; I can't sign something I haven't read. Possibly Mister Smyth might consent to summarize them for me."

"Mister Smyth is only here to witness your signature. He has no knowledge of their substance."

"Actually, My Lord, I have reviewed the documents and am completely familiar with their content."

"I don't care how familiar you are! Now sign the documents, Dina!"

"I shan't sign them. Grandfather, now if you'll excuse me, I must pack."

Lord Kimberly's shocked expression led to anger as Dina stood and turned toward the door to the library.

"Where do you think you're going?" His Lordship shouted. "I will tell you when you can go. Now, if you don't sit down and sign these papers, you can find another roof over your ungrateful head."

"Perhaps that is exactly what I intend to do, Grandfather.

"Good afternoon, Lord Smyth."

Chapter Two

Headlines meant little to Aaron; the month-old newspaper was barely legible anyway. He tossed the paper to the ground and glared at it. "As if anything mattered now," he said. The British were everywhere, so were the Germans and the Portuguese. They were easy targets, but there were just too many of them. The Dutch rebels continued to fight with all the passion and resolve you would expect, but their destiny would be determined on the floor of the House of Lords, not on the battlefields of South Africa. Defeat was a certain, everyone knew it; a few more rebels lying dead in the dirt wouldn't change anything.

Aaron wasn't alone; the remnants of what was once a formidable force were now huddled together; their bunker would not protect them much longer. He struggled for leverage using his rifle to pull him up the earthy slope and took one more look over the edge of the bunker. He could see the firelights from the British camp. By morning it would be over. There was nowhere to hide.

It wasn't that he regretted his decision; the ghetto was hell. No one blamed him, his parents or his fifteen brothers. The opportunity to leave Lithuania and the promise of land was more than enough motivation. The Paris Trading Company had offered free passage in exchange for five years of service. It wasn't clear what services he was to provide, and he really didn't care; anything was better than the ghetto.

Crouching low beneath the edge of the bunker, his hands covering his face, Aaron was alone in his thoughts. *I haven't seen my beloved Dina since my escape. She'd be eighteen now, a lady of grace and poise like her mother, no doubt. That was sixteen years ago; April 30, 1888.*

It all began when Barbara Kimberly became aware of Aaron's gaze; he'd been stowing some rigging at the bow when their eyes met. She was dressed in off-white lace and held an umbrella, twirling it as she walked along the dock. She looked up and saw him looking down at her. Suddenly, she caught the heel of her shoe between the wooden planks and fell to her knees, almost simultaneously pushed aside by a man carrying a large crate. She tried to get up and regain her balance but was hit from another passing crewman and thrust over the side and into the water. Aaron didn't hesitate. It was at least thirty feet, but Aaron dove to the rescue.

Before he had stepped foot in Cape Town, South Africa, he had dove off the end of his ship to save the life of the daughter of the most important man in the entire country.

What was I to do? What would any man do? How could I have known who she was? I could never have known. What if I had known? Does anyone think I would have found a way to meet and marry the daughter of the wealthiest man in Africa? How ridiculous is that? Who could have imagined that one day I would be rubbing shoulders with those Jew hating bastards?

The entire dockside was suddenly crowded with people frantic with concern over the attempted rescue. Two soldiers restrained Aaron as the semiconscious young woman lay on the dock, her head resting on the lap of her most trusted handmaiden.

"Oh, mistress!" she cried. "Please wake up. Please, mistress, please, oh please!"

"Stop the fussing, Tawney," Barbara said, as her eyes opened. "Can't you see I'm fine?"

Aaron was immediately impressed; a girl so obviously fragile and refined had just escaped drowning and was now passing it off as if it were nothing for which to be concerned.

The young heiress stood and defiantly addressed the two soldiers still holding Aaron.

"Release that man! Are you idiots? That man saved my life!" she shouted.

"Thank you, sir. That was very brave," she said, as Aaron helped her back to the carriage.

"I'm glad you're all right, miss."

Barbara looked around to find the unlikable Douglas Franks staring at them.

"Mister Franks! Please see to it that this brave man is escorted to the house where he can dry off and rest."

"No need, miss," Aaron said. "I have everything I need onboard."

"Don't be absurd; you have done a worthy deed and I intend to reward you for it, as will my father. Now come with me."

"I'm at your service," he said, making a short but appropriate bow.

"I don't even know your name," she said. "In the confusion and all, please forgive me."

"Uh, Rose, miss. Aaron...Rose."

Barbara was more handsome than pretty. She was only twenty, the only child of Lord and Lady Randolph Kimberly, a name synonymous with wealth born from the backs of poor miners digging for diamonds in the mines of South Africa. It was more than her knowing smile and sophistication that drew him to her. She was so young, but what intrigued him the most was her way of taking charge; even her own father dare not disappoint her.

Aaron had never been much of a ladies' man, thirty-five years old and still a bachelor. He had had little time for woman back in the ghetto. More than once he refused the attempts by the neighborhood matchmaker to marry him off to a nice Jewish girl. Unlike his brothers, Aaron avoided as best he could being shackled to a woman who would be more married to five thousand years of history than to him.

Lord Kimberly, the pompous self-appointed ruler of the colony, waited on the front steps of the mansion as Barbara's carriage came to a stop.

"Are you hurt, my dear?" His expression of concern was most sincere.

"No, Father. I'm quite all right, thanks to Mister Rose, here."

"Ah, yes, Mister Rose. I've been informed of your heroics, sir. There will be a banquet in your honor this evening. Please come in and refresh yourself."

That evening Aaron stood at the entrance to the dining room; the opulent table arrangement was unfamiliar; he never imagined such finery even existed. The handmade linen napkins, the crystal and gold-stemmed glasses, and flatware matched perfectly with the diamond jewelry on every hand, ear and neck of the invited elite. Amazingly, Aaron Rothberg, a.k.a. Aaron Rose, an indigent Jew from Lithuania, was now sitting shoulder to shoulder with what was surely a branch of South Africa's royal family.

Lord Kimberly stood at the head of the table with glass in hand.

"A toast, everyone! To the gallant and quick-minded Mister Rose, to whom I owe more than I can say. If not for him, my greatest joy might have been taken from me forever. Thank you, sir. To Mister Rose, everyone!"

"Mister Rose!" came from all thirty or so guests.

"Speech, sir, a few words, please," said the diamond merchant.

"Lord Kimberly and distinguished dinner companions, I am delighted with having the good fortune to share in this celebration. I am overcome by Your Lordship's generosity and am honored to have met all of you. I am a man who has traveled far, but never have I seen such kindness given to a stranger. I also lack the words to describe the joy you must feel, My Lord, but I can say this, if it was fate that chose me to be Miss Barbara's rescuer, then it is a fate for which I will always feel blessed; thank you, sir."

To some it seemed a little too dramatic, but to Barbara, Aaron's speech confirmed the possibility he might be just the kind of man who could talk his way into her father's heart, as well as his fortune.

After saying good night to her guests, Barbara led Aaron out onto the stone terrace that bordered the mansion's manicured gardens.

"I think you do an excellent impersonation of a "royal," she said. "Have you studied acting or does it just come naturally?"

They descended the stone stairs and walked together among the flowers in the candlelit garden.

Aaron was eager and willing just to listen. Barbara spoke to him about things that mattered to her. She could not care less that her father was an outspoken advocate of an independent South Africa. After her mother died five years earlier, she was without the only person in whom she ever confided. Her seemingly attentive father rarely spoke to her, and she couldn't remember ever being alone with him.

"What about you, Aaron, are you always this talkative?" she asked. His reluctance to talk about himself made him more curious and interesting. *It is his ruggedness, or is it something else*? There was a darkness about him, and his face seemed larger than normal; was it his eyes or the deep lines in his forehead?

Tawney called from above the stone terrace. "You there, mistress?" It was the beckoning that changed the mood from one of quiet questioning to one of urgency. He embraced her, never taking his eyes from hers. They stood holding each other, no longer strangers but passionate lovers. Pulled from the sea only hours before, they were now desperately reaching out for life.

Aaron returned to the mansion the following morning no longer employed by the Paris Trading Company. He had been successful in finding and altering the ship's documents earlier that night. Now Mister Aaron Rose had been simply a passenger on board a ship, and Mister Aaron Rothberg never ever existed.

"Mister Rose is here, My Lord."

"Send him in, Franks."

"Will there be anything else, My Lord?"

"No, Franks. See that we are not disturbed."

"Yes, My Lord."

Franks was more than just a house servant. His huge frame and intense stare made Aaron uncomfortable; he was glad to see him close the doors to His Lordship's library as he backed away and left.

"We have been impressed by your bravery, sir," he said. "We can use brave men in Africa."

His Lordship spoke for more than an hour. Aaron said little, just enough to indicate his understanding and sympathy for the plight of the wealthy Dutch, German and British businessmen who were on the brink of losing their fortunes to the British Crown.

"Are you disposed to consider an offer to work for us, Mister Rose?"

"What exactly would I be doing, sir?"

"Never mind that now. I would like you to accompany me to our offices, and if we can come to terms, you can accompany Franks to the mines."

Aaron may have thought there was nothing worse than life in the ghetto, but as he looked down into the cavernous pit and watched black men, young and old, scratching and clawing through the ochre earth, he realized this was surely a greater hell. Thousands of them were struggling, knowing that if they fell, it could be to their death.

"A magnificent sight, don't you agree, Rose?" Franks stared into Aaron's eyes and waited for an answer.

"It's very impressive, Franks."

"We have over a thousand blacks working this mine; each one of them is grateful to His Lordship."

"Grateful?" Aaron's amazement at the word didn't go unnoticed.

"Yes!" he said, not hiding his disdain. "His Lordship feeds them and provides each family with a house of their own; we don't hold with slavery, anymore."

If that isn't slavery I don't know what is. How could anyone not see the pain and horror these poor people are being subjected to? Aaron couldn't and didn't say another word all the way back to Cape Town.

"It is more than I can bear, Barbara! I have faced death many times and nothing has horrified me more. I will tell your father tomorrow it's impossible."

Barbara seldom, if ever, felt the need to enter her father's library, but the following morning she walked in unannounced.

"What is it, Barbara; can't you see I'm busy?"

"Leave us, Franks!" she said. Franks slowly did as he was told.

"You will find my fiancé a position befitting his stature; he is not interested in diamonds. Is that clear, Father?"

"Fiancé!" Lord Kimberly's shocked expression did nothing to soften Barbara's resolve. "You don't even know the man! How can you possibly be serious?"

"I know that I love him, and that is enough! You will announce our engagement this evening. Good day, Father."

They were married five weeks later. His Lordship had no choice but to agree; Barbara didn't have to remind her father that it was her mother's family who financed the entire mining business; upon her mother's death, Barbara became the owner of fifty-one percent of everything.

After a three-month honeymoon in England, the newlyweds took up residence in the old family home just outside Johannesburg. A month after that came the announcement that Barbara was expecting.

Diana (Dina) Penelope Rose was born on April 30, 1886. Aaron and Barbara Rose were sharing a dream—a dream that was precarious.

It was the afternoon of Dina's second birthday. Aaron and Barbara, Lord Kimberly and a few friends sat in the small dinning room while Dina stood on her father's chair at the head of the table quite content and admiring a new doll.

"Excuse me, Mister Rose," interrupted the butler. "Mister Franks is waiting outside with another gentleman. They wish to speak to you, in private."

"Tell Franks to come back later; we're too busy, aren't we, my darling?" Aaron smiled and continued dotting over his precious daughter.

"That's him all right!"

Aaron pushed back his chair and stood to face the uninvited officers.

"What's the meaning of this, Franks?" His Lordship demanded.

"I believe these gentlemen have something to say about Mister Rose, My Lord."

The taller of the two stepped forward and pointed at Aaron.

"He was on board. I remember him, and he's no gentleman! He's just a Jewish farmer who owes five years service to the Paris Trading Company. I hold the documents to prove it. This man is a fraud. His real name is Aaron Rothberg, a Jew from Lithuania."

Franks was obviously pleased with his efforts to expose Aaron; he stood next to him and looked at the diamond merchant waiting for instructions.

"Lies, all lies!" Barbara stood up and ordered Franks out of the house. "And take this liar with you," she screamed.

"Now, Barbara," said her father, "maybe you should ask Aaron if there is any truth to these allegations. Well, Aaron, what say you?"

Aaron's sudden grayness and pleading eyes had already betrayed him. Barbara held both hands to her throat and collapsed to the floor, striking her head on the sharp corner of the table, opening a massive wound behind her ear. Blood was pouring out onto the marble floor.

"For God's sake, someone fetch a doctor!" Aaron shouted. It was too late. Barbara was already dead. It wasn't the fall that killed her; the embolism had been there all along. It was only a matter of time before it would have hemorrhaged on its own.

Aaron listened to the sound of a thousand marching troops as the British infantry moved up the hill towards his position. *A fitting end. I might have been better off if I had let Franks kill me right then and there.* Aaron and the others moved to defend their bunker. A minute later, Aaron Rothberg, a.k.a. Aaron Rose, lay wounded and unconscious under a mound of fallen patriots.

It was May 1, 1904.

Chapter Three

Trefka was a typical Russian village; on one side of the river, the goyem; on the other the Jews—there was never any question who was better off. The Russians had a market, schools and churches. The Jews had nothing that resembled either.

Each day the farmers, bakers and butchers wheeled their carts into the center of town expecting everything to be sold by noon, leaving the rest of the day for prayer and study.

As the only blacksmith in the village, Avrahm Geller had little time to spend in synagogue. Avrahm had only one non-Jewish customer, and it made him feel safer knowing the Russian captain liked him. It was only yesterday the captain said, "You're a good man, Avrahm."

Avrahm removed his hat and wiped his brow. After replacing his hat just so, he raised his eyes to the ceiling.

"Let this be a lesson to you, Lord; don't make another *one* of anything."

"If you stopped selling yourself to the devil, maybe you would have the time to spend at temple." The old rabbi reached for his insubordinate son-in-law's arm and squeezed as hard as he could. "If God wanted you to serve the goyem, he would have made you one of them; don't you understand?"

"And if God wanted me to catch fish, he would have made me one of them, I suppose?" Avrahm was always courteous but his father-in-law had a way of getting under his skin.

The old rabbi finally let go of Avrahm's arm.

"You realize our enemy, the Tsar, has declared that all Jews are inhuman and should be slaughtered for manure."

"I'm sure the Tsar has more than enough manure, don't you think, Zeyda?" Avrahm was losing his patience.

"You will think differently after your Russian captain cuts off your head and feeds it to his horse, won't you, Avrahm?"

Rabbi Emmanuel Cohen's face hardened as he pointed and shook a crooked finger at his son-in-law.

"There is a minion in the morning; don't be late!" he said, kicking his heel into the dry dirt. "Good Shabbos, Avrahm!"

"And a very good Sabbath to you, Rabbi."

The centuries of oppression and slavery were a constant reminder. No Jew was really safe. Only God could protect you; and he would, provided you obeyed God's law. Each man and boy was expected to study the Talmud and honor its laws. Avrahm never understood it; if the Talmud was meant to be obeyed, why did his father-in-law and the other elders feel the need to debate its teachings.

The late afternoon sun made it impossible for Avrahm to see anything but the dark outline of the Russian. He had been standing watching the blacksmith for a couple of minutes.

"Is that you, Captain?" Avrahm asked.

"Yes, Avrahm, it is. Is my mount ready?"

"Yes, Captain. I'll bring him out right away."

Captain Peter Strovachev had been chief constable of Trefka for two years. In that time no Jew had been executed. He knew that pogroms were initiated by ruthless men, men he had met in Moscow, men without an ounce of charity. Men who killed for the joy of watching others suffer. "They need to be punished for killing Christ," they said. They all agreed except for Captain Strovachev.

"Surely, none who killed Christ is still alive," he said. The next thing he knew he was off to Trefka, his punishment for expressing sympathy for the Jews. He didn't care for them really; except for Avrahm, they were all just too intense for his liking. Avrahm had a wonderful sense of humor, one Peter looked forward to experiencing at least once a week.

"Ah, Avrahm, tell me; how is the charming Missus Geller lately? Is she causing you anymore aggravation, my friend?"

"I'm sorry, Captain, I don't recognize the name. Perhaps we better ask the gypsies; maybe…possibly…hopefully…they may have captured her."

"Now, Avrahm, is that any way to talk about your devoted wife?"

"You're right of course, Captain. I'm truly blessed. A devoted wife is hard to come by—I only wish I hadn't found one so easily."

"And what about your lovely daughters, surely they are a true blessing?"

"A burden I wouldn't wish on my worst enemy!" he said, smiling.

This was a lie of course; his daughters were his life. Nothing in the world was more important than Rachel and Besrah.

He called her Bessy; so tiny and so perfect. She was the smallest child in the village and everyone adored her. Just thirteen and she had already earned the respect of the entire village. She was always helping anyone who needed it. Her presence in the village made people forget the years of living in fear. Her heart-shaped face with dark blue eyes was the face on an ivory cameo, but alive. Rachel was more like his devoted wife; it wasn't that he didn't love her; she was just so serious about everything. She scolded him more often than his wife Sarah did. *She'll make a fine wife for someone, I'm sure.*

Captain Strovachev mounted his newly shod horse, took the reins in gloved hands and expertly backed the black mare out of the barn and onto the street.

"Give my regards to your family, my friend, especially the tiny one."

"I will, my captain, I will."

Avrahm and Peter were two of the most unlikely men to be friends; other than they both had left Lithuania around the same time, they had little in common. It was more like an understanding than a friendship; a young, handsome soldier and an overweight, middle-aged Jew—who would think?

Avrahm locked the door to the barn and started his journey home. It would be sundown soon; he didn't need another scolding.

Fridays brought new life to the otherwise quiet village. People scurried around making last minute preparations. Wives and daughters were cooking and polishing silverware—silverware that had been in their families for generations. Children were protesting their weekly bath.

It was just over a mile along the narrow road leading toward the setting sun. He would have to hurry, but promising his old mare not to ride her home on the Sabbath, well, he just couldn't break a promise, not on the Sabbath.

"Hello, Avrahm. Good Sabbath to you." Avrahm must have said "Good Sabbath" a hundred times before reaching the end of the street.

"Shabbat shalom, Mister Geller," the ten-year-old boy said, almost falling into Avrahm's arms as he ran across the dirt road in front of him.

"You should have built your house in the village, Geller!" the bent-over old woman shouted from the boardwalk.

"I know, I know, thank you for reminding me." *The Yenta*—Avrahm never liked her—always butting into other people's business. The old woman scratched out a living arranging marriages for anyone over the age of thirteen. It was as if she believed God Himself had chosen her. "My husband died so I could find husbands for everyone else." *She must say it a million times a day.*

Clouds of red dust rose over the rickety old wooden houses as Avrahm turned and looked once more down the road to the village. *Not much to look at, oh well, if God wanted me to live in a castle he would have made me King.* Avrahm laughed out loud, took a deep breath and held it before letting it out. *Maybe I should have built my house in the village.*

"Papa, Papa!" Bessy ran to him and wrapped her arms halfway around his waist and rested her head on his stomach. "Papa, Papa, I thought you would never get here." Avrahm caressed held her tiny head. "Momma is frantic, Papa. We better hurry. We're having an enormous goose, Papa!"

Sarah stood at the front door with her hands on aproned hips, glaring at him.

"So, you decided to come home; I thought maybe you got lost again. You could have built your house in the village like a normal person, you know."

"I know, I know already."

The family of four sat at the linen-covered table with their heads bowed while Sarah lit the candles and said the blessing.

"Amen," they said in unison.

"Now, let's see if this goose is as advertised." Avrahm carved the goose with precision; he was a master at it, so he believed.

"Papa?" Bessy was always the first to speak.

"Yes, my darling, what can I do for you?"

"Papa, did you know that Mister Tosker has a nephew visiting from Kiev, and Missus Stein, the matchmaker, well, she wants me to meet him. I don't think I want to meet him, Papa. What do you think?" Bessy reached for her father's hand. "Papa, is it true there are buildings in Kiev that reach the clouds, Papa?"

"Quiet, Besrah! Can't you see our father is trying not to cut off a finger?" Sarah smiled at her eldest daughter's remark.

"Papa?"

"Yes, Bessy. What?"

"Is fishing allowed on the Sabbath? I want to go fishing in the river with you, Papa. Can we do it tomorrow, Papa?"

"I don't think God will mind. Do you, my dear?" Avrahm glanced sheepishly at his frowning wife.

"There are things to do around here; things your father has been promising to do since before you were born. I think it's about time he did them, don't you, my husband?"

"Good idea, my love, fishing can wait." Bessy smiled and winked back at her wonderful father.

It was almost sunrise when Besrah bent over the bed and whispered into her father's ear, "Papa, wake up. We're going to miss the fish."

Sarah loved her beautiful daughter, and she loved Avrahm in spite of how she treated him. How she admired their relationship; they were more like playmates than father and daughter. She smiled into her pillow and pretended to sleep as the two of them snuck out still believing they hadn't been heard.

"Good morning, Avrahm!" Bessy squeezed her father's hand tight as Captain Strovachev greeted them on the road to the river.

"Good morning, Captain. It's a fine day, don't you think?"

"I do indeed, I do indeed. And who is this stranger next to you? I don't recall seeing anyone as pretty walking on this road before. Do you remember me, little Besrah?" The captain dismounted and knelt down in front of her.

"I certainly do, Captain," she said with her usual smile.

"And I remember you, too. Your father and I are friends, little Besrah. Would you like to be my friend?"

"My father likes you so…I guess I do too. You do like him, right, Papa?"

"Your papa has told me a lot about you, Bessy."

"I hope he told you only the good things, Captain."

Bessy tugged on her father's arm. "We will miss the fish, Papa."

"Yes, darling, we must be on our way. Captain, the fish are waiting."

The captain needed only one hand to mount the seventeen-hand mare.

"My name is Captain Strovachev, Bessy, but you can call me Peter. Maybe we will speak again. Good morning to you both." Besrah and Avrahm watched as the good captain galloped away.

"You do like him, don't you, Papa?"

"Yes, my sweet. The captain is a good man."

It was approaching sundown the following Friday as Avrahm lowered the hind leg of Mister Tosker's horse. *Sarah will be madder than a crow; why Tosker needed his horse shod today I cannot imagine. Now he hasn't the decency to show up to retrieve the old nag. I'm going to have to feed her now. This is going to cost him double.*

The week had gone so fast; he couldn't remember being so busy. Avrahm poured some oats into the trough and led the old horse into a stall at the back of the barn. Outside a pistol shot pierced the air. He heard another and then another. Quickly he ran to the front of the barn and peered out onto the deserted street. The usual Friday night throng of well-wishers had vanished. Another shot and a woman's scream came from the other end of the village.

Avrahm pulled himself up and onto the back of the old mare. More shots and another woman screamed. He sat hunched over the old mare and slowly made his way around to the back of the barn and along the uneven ground towards the other end of the village. The small synagogue was aflame and so were several other houses that lined the street on either side.

"Where is the priest? Which one of you Christ killers is the priest?" shouted the Russian sergeant. Thirty Russian soldiers on horseback had surrounded twenty or more villagers in front of the burning synagogue.

"I am the rabbi!" Avrahm's father-in-law, defiant as ever, stepped out of the crowd.

"No, Father, come back!" Sarah screamed.

"Zeyda, Zeyda! Come back!" Bessy shouted.

Avrahm's family, everything he loved in the world, was only a few feet away; how could he save them? Where was his friend, the captain? Why had he not been by the shop?

A Russian soldier pulled Avrahm backward off the old mare and dragged him across the dirt road and tossed him in front of the other villagers.

"Let this be a warning to all of you!" the angry Russian shouted. "We don't want any more Jewish priests!"

The Russian pointed his pistol and shot the old rabbi in the chest. Sarah ran to him and fell over him screaming.

"You animals! Why? He was just an old man."

Without hesitation, the Russian recocked his pistol and fired twice more, killing Sarah and Avrahm.

"No! No! Papa! Mamma!" Bessy ran from her sister's arms and collapsed over her dead parents' bodies. The Russian reached for his pistol once again but his arm was caught from behind before he could find the handle.

"There has been enough killing today, don't you think, Sergeant? Now, return to your unit immediately," Peter Strovachev ordered angrily. "I will finish up here!

"I have my orders to kill five," said the sergeant.

"I have my orders as well! Now, tell your men to leave, or I will have to report you for disobeying an order from a superior officer. Now go!"

Reluctantly, the Russians holstered their pistols and left. Peter Strovachev knelt beside the weeping child and comforted her.

"Come now, little Besrah, I will look after you now."

Chapter Four

"Your name, what the hell is your name, sir?"

The immigration man was sitting at a long table with two other officials. Aaron turned and looked at the hundreds in line behind him and thought about the thousands who had already landed in Montreal that day. Many were denied entry and many were treated like criminals and simply thrown into dungeons to await their fait. Aaron arrived without papers of any kind; his fortunate survival and ship passage to Canada had been provided by an unknown source. He had only the clothes on his back, no money and no idea how he was going to survive. The only thing he did have were the memories of a broken heart and a broken dream, made worse by the unrelenting headaches that would plague him for the rest of his life.

"This is your last chance; what the hell is your name?" Aaron shook his head and tried to focus.

"Ah, Roth. Aaron Roth."

"Occupation. Occupation"

"Farmer. Farmer."

"Religion. Religion."

"Jewish. Jewish."

"Are you getting smart with me, Jew?"

"No, sir! Not me."

"You better not be, if you want to survive, Jew. Next!"

Ten hours standing in line only to be thrown into a holding cell for who knew how long. Aaron sat on the stone floor with his head between his knees. It was hard not to think about what brought him to this place. The city of Montreal and the prospect of a new life didn't stop the pain of the past. Everything was gone. The life he had built after escaping from the diamond merchant was over. The land he toiled over for sixteen years, also gone. His beloved wife dead and a daughter he would never see again.

Aaron wanted to cry. He couldn't remember the last time he had cried; perhaps he had never cried.

"That's him, over there! The one on the floor, crying," said the jailer.

"Thank you, jailer. That will be all."

The distinguished looking gray-haired gentleman stood over Aaron and spoke in a calm and deliberate manner.

"Are you Aaron Rothberg?" he asked. Aaron slowly looked up.

"Yes, I'm Roth."

"My name is Straith, William Straith. I work for Mister Jacob Rothberg, your brother. Please, come with me."

It wasn't the most joyous of reunions. Although neither brother had the slightest notion of why or how this incredible coincidence happened, neither seemed to care. The possibility never occurred to either of them that this quirk of fate would do anything to change what must be done. To have the opportunity to assist a brother in his time of need was a blessing both recognized and understood.

Jacob had come to Canada fifteen years earlier with only his wits and a desire to be the richest man alive. From liquor salesman to the owner of the largest brewery in Quebec, Jacob Rothberg had accomplished much. Sadly, he lost his wife to scurvy on the journey from Lithuania. Now, still unmarried and no children, his only motivation, other than money, was his dedication to the synagogue—which he not only built and paid for, but as chairman allowed himself to allocate all available congregational funds to assist thousands of European Jews wanting to immigrate to Canada.

Being reunited with his youngest brother wasn't turning out to be such a blessing. Jacob was not happy that his brother refused to attend temple services, and he felt Aaron wasn't interested in becoming part of the local Jewish community. When his rudeness became the talk of the congregation, Jacob was forced to take action. Fortunately for Aaron, a new law was passed granting homestead rights to married immigrants, and Jacob immediately seized the opportunity.

"Aaron," he said, "you need a wife!"

"You must be crazy!" Aaron protested.

"Aaron, if you get a wife, you get four hundred acres of fertile Alberta farmland."

Aaron actually longed for the farmer's life again. The prospect of owning another farm, wife and all, was a far better fate than anything Montreal had to offer.

"Well, brother," Aaron asked, "how do I get a wife?"

The door to Jacob's office opened and a small but beautiful young woman walked in. "Allow me to introduce you; this is Besrah Geller."

"Hello," she said, smiling up at him. "My name is Besrah, but you can call me Bessy."

The last thing from his mind before now was a wife; but after careful consideration of his remaining options, he took the advice and the hand of Besrah Geller in marriage.

By covered wagon, Aaron and Bessy Roth journeyed across the northern frontier of Canada. If he had timed it right, they would arrive in Grand Prairie, Alberta, just in time to till and plant the first year's crops.

"Scat, Bartholomew, you rascal. Can't you see I'm busy?" The bear cub was relentless as he continued to claw and pull at Bessie's apron. "All right already, I'll give you something."

"It won't be much, Bartholomew." Rachel hadn't lost her touch.

"That isn't particularly funny, Rachel," she said.

"Oh, Bess, you know I'm kidding."

"You have never kidded a day in your life, my dear sister." Rachel's expression hardened.

"I know. I see how he treats you. You weren't supposed to be a farmhand for the master. There were plenty of young, rich men who would have snatched you up, if you had just given them a chance."

"I must say, dear sister, your attitude is less than tolerant."

"Tolerant! What would Papa have said if he knew you married an old man from nowhere?"

Bessy wouldn't think about the horror that took her parents. Only her beloved captain stayed in her thoughts. If not for him, she and her sister would never have survived. *God bless my captain.*

"There is nothing you can say, my dear sister, that will change my mind. Oh, and another thing, I'm pregnant."

"What?" exclaimed Rachel. "How did that happen? Did he rape you? You can tell me, Bessy, I'm your sister."

"That is simply not the case. Perhaps you would like one more piece of cake before you leave?"

Aaron didn't fool her. Rachel saw what a brute he was. She blamed herself; it was she who gave them permission to marry in the first place; she and the kind Mister Rothberg, of course, poor man. Rachel had traveled all the way from Regina to see her sister, and now that she had, she wished she hadn't. There was nothing she could do, and as a result of her effort to extricate her sister from the farmer's clutches, she opened a wound that would never heal. Bessy was steadfast in her resolve to build a life even in this desolate place; she would endure whatever God had in store for her, and she would do it no matter what.

Bessy stood on the steps of the small farmhouse and gazed over the gentle slopes of the Peace River country. Next week she would start preparing for her first of thirteen winters; soon a blanket of ice would cover the land for a thousand miles in every direction.

Aaron didn't hide his disappointment. All winter long he complained about just about everything. Finding fault in Bessy was his way of passing time. In spite of this, she was certain there was a warm and kind person somewhere underneath. She never spoke harshly to her husband; she thought it would only serve to further anger him. She was right of course, and as time passed Aaron began to see in his little wife a person far more capable to deal with hardship than he was. Nothing he said could discourage her from being exactly as she had always been, the tiniest person with the kindest of hearts

Emanuel (Manny) was born in April 1913, then Dina in the same month three years later. Aaron never explained to Bessy after whom Dina was named. Emanuel was her beloved grandfather's name. It was customary to name your children after your closest dead relative, but Aaron had insisted, and of course Bessy didn't argue. But as time went by Bessy became far less inclined to obey her aging and insensitive husband.

"You must speak English, Bessy," he said. "It's very important. Our children need to speak English; you understand, don't you?"

"I understand I've lived here for thirteen years. I understand I have to provide a home for my family, and I understand the importance of teaching our children the languages of their ancestors. I can speak English; it's not so difficult. I speak Russian and Lithuanian better than you do."

"Fine, fine, I give up." Aaron threw his hands up only to let them fall again as Bessy patted the back of his head. "That boy of yours is late again," he said. "He's probably hanging around with that Penner kid."

Dina jumped into Manny's arms and climbed over his head and onto his back, turning and twisting around him. She always waited at the end of the road for her brother to come home from school.

"C'mon, Manny, let's go!" she shouted.

"OK, we're going now; hold on tight."

Manny ran up the dirt road towards the house as Dina bounced up and down on his back.

"Wait one second," he said, letting Dina get off only long enough to put down his paper parcel. "OK, once more around and this bird is going to the moon."

"Wheeeee!" Dina screamed, as the two of them ran and jumped in the open area between the house and the barn.

"Manny!" Aaron's voice rang out from the veranda.

"Yes, Father?"

"Have you got the meat for the Sabbath?"

A sudden dread swept over the thirteen-year-old. It was a feeling he knew very well.

It wasn't that Aaron disliked his son; he just didn't know what to do with him. He was so small, like his mother. He couldn't do the work in the fields that a normal-sized boy could do. He just wasn't strong enough and besides, he had no sense of responsibility—always joking and playing tricks on everyone. Not the kind of boy of which Aaron could ever be proud. He was just so damn small.

Though Manny was eager to please his father and more than willing to hunt and fish with him, Aaron seldom gave him the opportunity. Manny could do nothing right; his little mistakes, normal for any child, were dealt with in the only way his father knew how, he beat him—in fact, it was routine. After Manny did something wrong, he would, without being told, head out to the tool shack behind the barn and waited for his father and his beating. It was as if he believed he needed to be beaten, so he could be strong like his father.

Dina was a completely different story. She was tiny like her mother. Although her name was meant to remind him of his first child, she was nothing like her. She was strong-minded and never let her difficult surroundings prevent her from being happy. Manny adored her; she made him forget how cruel his father was. After each beating Dina opened the door to the tool shack and, as if nothing had happened, would draw him out and plead with him to start a new adventure.

"C'mon, Manny, it will be dark soon. You don't want to miss the train to New York, do you?" she asked.

Aaron looked sternly into his young son's eyes.

"Tell me you didn't lose the meat. Go on; tell me you haven't spoiled the Sabbath!"

"I had it. I put it down and..."

Bartholomew crept up onto the porch, and standing on his hind legs, displayed the butcher paper stuck to his front paw. Upon seeing this, Aaron immediately turned and went into the house, returning a moment later holding his rifle. He pointed it and fired, killing Bartholomew.

It was one thing for Aaron to beat her son. It was another thing to hurt an animal. Bessy loved animals and they loved her. The farm was a refuge for every stray bear or bobcat. Bartholomew was her favorite; she found him and raised him from only days after he was born.

She was furious and screamed at her husband for the first time in her life. Aaron's anger over the meat was nothing compared to Bessy's. She used a wooden spoon and beat him over the head and shoulders as she chased him around the house screaming, "You monster; you try and come into this house again I'll shoot you, you bastard. I will never forgive you!"

Immediately, Aaron turned his anger and frustration towards his son.

"This is all your fault!" he yelled. "Get out to the shack, right now!"

Manny was shivering in the tool shack as little Dina opened the door.

"Manny! Oh, Manny! Papa, Papa's dead."

Aaron Rothberg, a.k.a. Aaron Rose, dead from a heart attack at seventy-six years of age.

Chapter Five

It was 1933. Manny Roth was twenty. It was a difficult lesson, but Manny's reputation for hard work earned him the respect he never got from his father. After a wealth of experience in an assortment of jobs, Manny borrowed some money, moved east and started a small but profitable dry goods agency with his best friend. Before you knew it, the frightened child had become a budding entrepreneur.

"Hello, Sal," Manny said, as he entered Gold's general store.

The six-foot-seven Russian was placing cans of olive oil on the shelf behind the counter but stopped, turned and looked down at the top of Manny's bald head.

The tall white-haired Russian immigrant was Manny's most troublesome customer. He was always complaining that his order was short, and he never paid his bill on time. Manny was not supposed to take this matter up with the enormous Russian; his partner Seth was far better suited to deal with him. Seth never lost his temper and could turn an argument into laughter faster than anyone.

"So, Roth, how's Sudbury's youngest," he was going to say shortest, "businessman, today?"

"No use complaining, Sal, who would listen?"

"You're a funny guy, Roth, a real barrel of laughs."

"Yep, that's me, Sal. Speaking of barrels, I need a barrel of olive oil for Missus Schneider's new eatery. Oh, and, Sal, would you mind putting it on account?"

"Sure, Manny."

"Oh, and by the way, Sal, I'm having difficulty collecting my overdue accounts. Tell me, Sal, what do you do when your accounts are left unpaid?"

"Well, to tell you the truth, I see them at the temple and I tell them I can't fill their next order. When they protest, I simply give them the look; you know, like this." Sal stretched out his massive arms and turned his palms up and shrugged. Manny stared into the Russian's eyes, stretched out his arms and turned his palms up.

"Like this, Sal?"

"You are one cocky guy, Roth. If you were bigger, I'd take you outside and…"

Before he could finish Manny jumped up onto the counter and tried to grab the Russian by the throat, but he was caught from behind and pulled backwards.

"You're right, Sal. Roth's days are numbered around here. It won't be long before no one is safe from this menace. I don't know what to do with him."

Manny glanced at Seth and quickly turned back to resume his efforts to get at the Russian.

"Let me at him, Seth! Just give me a minute with him. He'll pay us, or I'll take it out of his Russian carcass!"

Seth stepped in front and pretended to protect the Russian.

"Gee, Sal, I don't know if I can hold him back; maybe you better pay him before he goes berserk."

"All right, Penner, but you better get a leash for that crazy midget!"

It wasn't the first time the two friends left Sal Gold's store bent over in the street laughing. It was times like these that made Seth Penner Manny's favorite person in the world. Seth could make Manny laugh anytime he wanted, and Seth wanted to very much. They had been friends back in Grand Prairie since they were six. Seth witnessed firsthand the cruelty dished out by Manny's father and he would do anything to help Manny forget.

"I know you're the toughest two-foot-guy on the block, but, you know, sometimes I think you're really going to pop that guy. Yep, here he goes! I can't hold him! You're a goner, Gold!" Seth was pushing and rocking him from side to side as he led him up to the curb and the new Buick.

Across the street and down a block was S&M Dry Goods. The boyhood friends had started the business together two years earlier, and in spite of the depression were incredibly successful. They stocked and sold everything and anything. As long as there was a demand, the boys knew where to find it. Even the great Hudson Bay Company couldn't compete with them. In fact, S&M was one of their biggest suppliers.

Manny was still laughing out of control and banging his head on the dash of the royal blue roadster.

"Settle down, Manny, my boy. We're off to find the girl of my dreams—which will not happen if you're going to keep bashing your head against this beautiful piece of machinery like that."

"Stop it, Seth! I can't take any more."

"OK! OK! Which dive shall we honor with your presence tonight?"

Manny couldn't believe his good fortune; just twenty-two years old and well on his way to somewhere.

"We need to expand, Seth. We need to open our own retail stores. Nobody is better equipped than we are to compete with the biggies."

"Look, Manny, if you want a department store, go ahead. I won't stop you. Just count me out, OK?"

"Will you just think about it, Seth, please?"

"OK, I'll think about it, after our fall trip. Until then, I don't want to talk about it, all right?"

"All right, partner, after the fall trip."

Another year passed without mentioning department stores. Manny sensed his friend was just not interested, especially after such a successful season. The boys continued to establish themselves. They sold everything there was to sell. They represented several manufacturers and warehoused products for distribution to every city and town across eastern Canada. It was perhaps the greatest and most successful partnership of the times. Their customers seldom postponed or cancelled an appointment; if they did, they would have to make the trip to one of now three warehouses set up between Sudbury in the north and Ottawa and Toronto in the southeast. Manny brought in some of their Jewish customers to invest in his expansion plans, and they were happy to do it provided he spent the appropriate amount of time at temple. He did, and as a result established more close business relationships with other Jewish investors. The money was flowing in and so were the good times. The boys reputation had also grown in every honky-tonk bar and saloon from Toronto to Halifax.

"Hey, Manny, look!" The sign on the roof said Rothmans but only the first four letters were lit. "This is it, man!" Seth parked the forest green roadster directly in front of the door. "I heard this place really jumps, old buddy; it's got your name on it too."

It was just a cigarette sign; the name on the saloon door said Randy's.

"Set 'em up, barkeep; we're a couple of thirsty travelers," Manny said, as the boys took their seats at the bar.

She was polishing a glass with her back to them, facing the dark mirrored wall. She could see them but they couldn't see her. Without turning around, she wiped another glass and placed it on the counter along with several others.

"What'll it be, gents?" she asked, still with her back to them. Seth was quick to answer.

"A better look at you, darling. Until then, I'll have Crown Royal, water back."

She turned to face them as Manny tried to give his order.

"I'll have the..."

She was too beautiful for words. The boys just sat there on their respective stools, mouths open and speechless.

"C'mon, you can do it," she said. "S-a-m-e, that's it. Now just put your teeth together and say sssss.

Manny slowly started to make the s sound but the rest of the word wouldn't come out.

"He'll have the same. C'mon, boyo, pull yourself together. Do you want our bartender to think you're retarded or something?"

"My name is Randy, Randy Zwilling. I own the place." Seth could hardly control himself.

"You gotta be kidding. Zwilling! Is that really your name?"

"It sure is, sweetie. It is now anyway. It was my husband's name, and now its mine."

"Was?" asked Seth.

"Ya, the old guy just couldn't keep up; keeled over one night sitting on that very stool. Ben loved to dance the jitterbug, he did. I miss him a lot."

Manny couldn't take his eyes off her. He sat next to Seth still mute as a mouse until he saw it—a small gold Star of David hung around her neck.

"You're Jewish!"

Manny's sudden outburst rattled the glasses and brought numerous stares from the smattering of customers seated at tables at the far end of the bar.

"What, you never see a Jew before?" she asked.

"It's OK, darling, his grandfather was a rabbi."

The fact that a Jewish girl was working in this rundown joint didn't bother Seth, but Manny was in shock.

"I suppose you think all Jewish girls were meant only to cook and clean up after their holy husbands; well not me, buster. I'm sure your mamma held your hand and wiped your nose while you toiled over the Talmud." Randy had had enough. "Well, I know one thing for sure, I've got other customers. Maybe I'll see you boys some other time."

"C'mon, sport, I gotta get you to a doctor before your mouth falls off."

Later in his motel room, Manny tossed and turned, unable to sleep. They had left the bar just after nine. Now after midnight he found himself behind the wheel of Seth's roadster on his way along Highway Sixty, back to Randy's Saloon.

"You again," she said. "I thought I'd seen the last of you."

"I just wanted to apologize. I…I couldn't sleep knowing I had offended you; will you forgive me?"

"Sure, sweetie. What'll you have?"

Manny waited patiently as Randy said good night to the few remaining customers before finally sitting with him. They talked until three; he was still in awe but had become comfortable just listening and looking at her. She spoke about her family and how she had been thrown out of her father's house because she had been caught with a non-Jewish boy from school. She hadn't seen or heard from her brother or sister in ten years. On the run with no one to help her, Randy had fallen into a life of bad booze and bad men, sometimes resorting to prostitution just to survive. Ben Zwilling was more than twice her age the night he tried to throw her out of the bar; but by month's end he had saved her, loved her and married her. Five years later he dropped dead from a heart attack.

Her hair was as black as night; it glowed and shimmered from the reflections of light thrown from the table candles. Randy could tell Manny was extremely short, but she imagined without her heels she wasn't that much taller. His eyes explored every feature of her face; they darted back and forth from her purple lips to her dark green eyes. Her black dress revealed just enough to stir his desire while the necklace drew him to the outline of her bosom.

She felt safe with him, even seeing his embarrassment when she caught him starring at her breasts made him even more attractive. He seemed kind and was handsome to boot, and from what she could gather, pretty well off.

She hadn't had time to organize a better place to live; since Ben died she was living and sleeping in the back room of the saloon. Funny, this was the first time she had even considered entertaining a man for anything other than conversation.

Manny was sure she could hear his heart pounding.

"Would you like to see where I sleep?" she asked.

Even as the words came from her mouth, she couldn't believe she was saying them. They stood up simultaneously, their chairs screeching along the wooden floor. She held out her hand and led him down a dark hall at the back of the saloon.

A small lamp on a wooden table cast shadows of light over the bed and along the floor to the other side of the makeshift bedroom. Randy kicked off her high heels, turned and drew him to her.

Sure, there had been other girls; behind the Russian's store with the Vickers' daughter was the first. What a time to think of that. He quickly put it out of his mind. She held his face in her hands and kissed him. He lingered there as the kiss became deeper and more passionate. He held her tighter as the faint moan from inside her encouraged him to go forward. He cradled her head in his arm and looked deeply into her eyes. It was sudden but somehow expected. She slid her hand down over Manny's stomach, reaching his penis; she held it softly then expertly caressed and stroked its length. He moaned with delight; his breathing quickening until suddenly gasping as Randy's mouth had taken over.

Sex had been a part-time business with Randy; the idea that sex was something to enjoy never occurred to her until now. Her husband had been big and overweight; for all the reasons she loved him, sex was not one of them.

At sunup, Manny parked the roadster in front of Seth's motel room and honked

"You there, cowboy," Manny hollered. "We're going to New York City. Get your things; you're coming with us."

Seth opened the door and saw Manny and Randy sitting in the convertible grinning from ear to ear.

"What the heck?"

This might have been the only time in his life that Seth Penner was at a loss for words. He just simply gathered his clothes from the room, threw some money on the bed, walked out and jumped into the back seat of the roadster.

"Well," he said. "What kept you people, I've been up for hours."

Nineteen thirty-six: it was the golden age of songwriters and performers—men and woman who sang about love and romance. It was the lyrics back then, the ones you could really hear.

New York City and Broadway. The nightclubs and Harlem. The Ritz and the Copa Cabana. All three of them ate in Manhattan for breakfast; one week later and they were still going strong.

There was Sigfield and Jolson, Berlin and more; all the greats like Billie Holiday. The boys spent more money than they knew they had. Nothing was too good or too expensive; they had to have everything. Manny bought Randy every dress and every hat and every piece of jewelry she saw. If she was beautiful before, she was stunning now. A taste of the good life was all she needed.

"Where's our boy?" Seth asked.

Randy, cocktail glass in hand, was standing at the door to Seth's room wearing a black velvet robe and rocking her head from side to side, smiling.

"He's pooped and I'm not. Got a drink? Hic."

Manny lay face down in the pillow. Slowly at first, but then quickly, he ran his hand over the sheets next to him. She wasn't there. He threw a towel around his waist and walked around the penthouse suite. The light over the entrance was on and the door was open, as Manny walked out into the hallway and saw Seth's door open.

"Oh! Hello, shorty, you're up," she said, as she brushed right by him and staggered her way down the hallway towards their suite.

Seth stood bent over in the doorway as Manny approached.

"What the hell!" Manny shouted.

"Now, it's not what you think, Manny."

"Don't tell me what I think, you bastard!" Manny stepped back glaring at his friend. "You and I are through! I never want to see you again."

Randy lay on the sofa with one foot on the floor and her robe wide open as Manny stood over her, his anger growing inside of him.

"I should have known," he said. "I find a whore in a bar and I get exactly what I deserved. I loved you, you bitch."

She felt his anger but wouldn't move; *it is better this way*, she thought. Now she can go back to the bar where she belonged.

The next day Seth sat in the hotel dinning room peeking over the top of the morning paper and waiving for Manny to join him.

"Look, pal," he said. "She just wasn't worth it; we got too much going for a woman to break us up. We go back too long to let that happen, right, cowboy?"

"Right, Seth." Manny could feel the twinge of pain and despair but agreed with his best friend. "Yep, just not worth it."

Al Bloom felt pretty proud of himself. If not for him, Roth's Department Store would never have happened. It was three years ago when Canada's only Jewish mayor convinced a number of prominent Toronto Jews that Manny Roth was a man to be trusted. Sure, he was only twenty-five, but he was already more experienced in business than men twice his age. And besides, he put up fifty thousand of his own money, just like everyone else, except for the bank that gave Manny the two million.

"Looks great, Manny, everything looks great."

"I couldn't have done it without you, Al."

Manny and three other gentlemen stood just inside the main entrance of Roth's. The enormous chandelier glimmering twenty feet above them was breathtaking. The store was ten thousand feet on each floor, right in the center of town. Ottawa would never look the same again.

Manny walked up and down the aisles inspecting every display; in twenty minutes he would be open for business selling every conceivable product at prices no one could beat. That was Manny's gift; he knew how to buy and sell merchandise. His idea of smaller markups through mass volume was an inspiration. He found deals on things people couldn't do without and advertised it at an unbelievable price. People lined up before the doors opened. Of course, the idea being that once they were in the store they wouldn't leave without buying something. Manny Roth invented the loss leader.

"I want my customers to shop, not schlep," he said.

Seth hadn't any regrets about not being part of Roth's. It wasn't that he didn't think it would be successful, it was just that he wasn't ready to settle down. He needed and loved the life of a traveling salesman.

"Yep, pretty remarkable, buddy; now the biggest little guy in town, huh? One day, when I'm as old as you, pal, don't forget to look me up, OK?"

"OK, pal, I will."

Seth bought Manny out of S&M; everything was amicable but he was happy to let Seth go his own way. As for the memories of New York, they would never go away.

After three months it was obvious; Manny Roth and Roth's Department Store were on their way to success beyond anyone's dreams. At only twenty-six years of age, Manny Roth had become the most eligible bachelor in town.

The synagogue was packed; rows of people praying—or it appeared that way anyway. Actually, Friday night services were more of a social occasion than a religious event. Every girl in town dressed up in her finest clothes wanting to make the best impression she could on the wealthy Manny Roth. Today was a minor holiday and important enough to insure the ladies auxiliary had set out enough pastries and crustless sandwiches to feed the entire congregation.

"What a catch your brother is, Dina. You know, Dina, I have always felt something special for your brother. I was wondering if you might…"

"Listen, Lisa, if you want to talk to my brother, there he is."

Dina's friendship for her newest and best friend was waning as the old woman turned and stared at the two girls from the pew in front of them.

"Shush!" she scolded.

"But, Dina," Lisa whispered, "you could say just the right thing, and…"

"Please, Lisa, I am not a yenta."

It wasn't the first time Dina gave her girlfriends the brush off. She had promised Manny she wouldn't try and fix him up with anyone. He was too busy and had far more important things to do. Manny had already signed a contract to build two more stores, one in Oshawa and another in the thriving town of Belleville, east of Toronto. Manny Roth was now a very important man in the Jewish community as well as everywhere else. His office on the top floor of Roth's was always crowded with men looking for the next deal. Manny was constantly asked to sponsor community events, and as vice-chairman of Mayor Bloom's re-election committee, he had little time for anything else. His good looks and personality and his way of looking taller than five foot two had propelled him to the top of the social ladder. The fact that he was Jewish was constantly overlooked, even by the most conservative

Christian. After all, he employed more non-Jews than anyone in town. His latest charity would place him among the cities most benevolent citizens.

"In addition," the rabbi continued, "any and all donations to the Manny Roth Orphanage made after tonight will not be recognized on the wall of honor until next month. Also, I am happy to report, that construction on the orphanage will commence on Monday; the groundbreaking ceremony will start at nine a.m. Mayor Bloom will be there as will a number of government people. It will be very exciting."

The rabbi waited for silence as he raised his arms and held them over the congregation. "May the Lord bless you, and keep you, amen." The rabbi finished the benediction and leaned over to shake Manny's hand.

"We are all very proud, Manny. God will bless you for what you have done."

After services, Manny was standing in the back stairwell of the synagogue in conversation with one of his business associates when Bessy interrupted.

"Excuse us for a moment, Harold," she said.

"Of course, Besrah," said the middle-aged jeweler.

"Well, Manny, my son, it seems you've come along way. Hope you remember the little people who helped you, and don't forget to thank God."

"Yes, Momma, I won't forget."

Manny had bought both his mother and Dina homes in the best Jewish neighborhood and gave them enough money to guarantee both of them the opportunity to find husbands. It was uncanny to see both of them together. They looked more like sisters than mother and daughter. Bessy was being courted by a number of gentlemen, most of them confused about to whom they were more attracted, the mother or the daughter.

By January 1939, both were happily married. Bessy had found comfort in the doting arms of Max Fine, once a strong and virile man, now riddled with arthritis. Dina found a jovial fellow from Montreal named Bernie Sarin; not too bright but a heart as big as her own.

"I don't care how important you are," she continued scolding Manny, "God's laws must come first."

"Yes, Momma, I know, and I promise to walk to the store tomorrow. Now, I have to finish my talk with Mister Wine. I will call you later."

"Call, don't call, it's all the same to me," she said.

Harold Wine, along with Al Bloom, was among Manny's biggest supporters. But when it came right down to it, that support could come and go if Manny didn't play his cards right.

"If you front the deal, Manny, you can count all of us in," the jeweler said.

The proposition intrigued Manny. The West was opening up, abound with opportunities to expand Manny Roth's department store empire.

"Vancouver, huh? I'll give it some thought, Harold. I'll let you know by Monday, OK?"

"Sure, Manny, sure. In the mean time, I'll send a few wires."

Manny wasn't positive about Vancouver, but it was obvious that his colleagues would not be pleased if he refused. The following day Manny made his decision.

"I've thought about it," he said over the phone. "I'm willing to make the trip, but if the deal isn't right, I won't promise anything."

"Sure, Manny. Sure."

Chapter Six

"The most beautiful country in the world, don't you agree, young sir?"

The tall black porter now serving meals in the dinning car spread the linen napkin on Manny's lap and placed the brown leather bound menu on the table in front of him. The cover embossed in gold said *Canadian Pacific Rail.* The Canadian corporate establishment had already begun to sink its teeth into the riches of the West.

"I haven't seen the rest of the world," Manny said, "but I'm guessing we have the biggest country in the world, that's for sure."

Three days with nothing to do but look out the window. He hardly slept; the constant clackety clack from the train's wheels wouldn't allow it. When Manny did sleep it was never more than a couple of hours, and each time he did, the nightmares came, the same nightmares he had been having his whole life. He couldn't explain them even to himself. When he woke, the images would disappear and he would have no memory of them; only the headaches and the fear remained, fear of being punished for something he inevitably would do.

Manny woke around three and found the porter seated in the smoking room at the back of the sleeper car.

"Mind if I join you?" he asked.

"C'mon, don't pay no attention to me. I'll be a goin'."

The porter twisted the head off his cigarette into the metal ashtray and started to stand.

"No! Don't leave. I could use the company," Manny said.

"You sure? I'm not really supposed to be a sittin' here."

"Here, have one of mine." Manny opened his package of Export and offered one to the porter.

"Why, don't mind if I do. Got no store-bought aboard this here train."

The two men shared two more cigarettes; afterwards, they just sat quietly waiting for the other to speak. Manny listened to the porter tell stories of how his parents kept heading north to distance themselves from their slave masters.

"Canada's my home now; six months at home and six months on the trains. I'm a happy man, know what I mean?"

"I know what you mean," Manny said.

"You gotta raincoat, son?" the porter asked.

"I don't, no."

"Well you better git yourself one, before you drown. It's always a rainin' in Vancouver."

Leaving the station, Manny waived good bye to the porter. *Funny, I never asked his name.*

Manny hailed a taxi and got to his hotel about five, took a bath, had a shave and got a shoeshine downstairs. By nine he had eaten an excellent dinner. Before leaving, he asked the waiter for directions to the best nightclub in town.

"That would be the Palace," he said. "Two blocks down and to the left."

"Would you like a table, sir?" the tuxedoed maitre d' asked.

"No, I think I'll just have a seat at the bar, if that's all right?"

"Certainly, sir," he said, as Manny slipped the fiver into the man's hand.

"Thank you, sir; right this way."

He was well positioned; he could see over the tables to the dance floor and up to the stage behind. Several couples were dancing as a Benny Goodman look-alike waived his baton over them. There were people having dinner on a raised balcony that hung over the edge of the bar on the left, and there was another one on the right with people just talking and drinking. The people on the right were considerably louder than those on the left.

Manny noticed a group of women seated above. *They are obviously working girls*. After slipping another five to the maitre d', Manny took the seat at the table next to the noisy six.

Moments later he stood at the end of their table smiling.

"Good evening, ladies. My name is Manny. I was wondering if any of you charming ladies might consider a dance. Are you free, miss?"

She looked up at him then back at her friends, folded her napkin, placed it on the table then reached out and took Manny's hand.

"Mary!" her shocked sister exclaimed.

"Ta ta, Lillian. I'm sure Manny doesn't think he has to pay me, do you, Manny?"

"I..."

"Never mind, let's dance."

"Can I ask your name?" he asked, holding her at an appropriate distance.

"I'm sure you are quite capable of asking; didn't you hear my sister? Everybody else in the room did."

"Ah, yes. It's Mary, right?"

"You are the clever one, aren't you?" she said mockingly.

Boy, talk about your smart broads. Manny knew right off, that besides her being the prettiest girl in the room she was obviously the brightest. She wasn't that much taller than him, just an inch or two. She had huge blue eyes and dark brown hair that hung over her narrow shoulders. She felt fragile, yet the way she danced it was almost as if she was leading him.

Mary was pleased with herself; she could use a good laugh. It wouldn't be long before her father found out where she and her sister had gone.

The music stopped and Mary started back to her table.

"Wait a minute! You wouldn't grant a stranger one more dance with the prettiest girl in the room?" He caught her hand as she looked into his pleading eyes.

"You are a persistent fellow, I must say," she said.

"Please, Mary, just one more."

Mary placed her arm around his shoulder. The music hadn't started but she didn't notice; what she did notice was Manny—she hadn't really looked at him yet. He was dashing, short but handsome—and those spats. She really didn't care for mustaches but on Manny she thought it looked good.

One more dance led to two, then three. They didn't talk much, just danced, but their thoughts were exploring endless possibilities.

Back at the table, Mary made more formal introductions.

"Ladies," Mary said, "this is Manny Roth. He's visiting from Ontario. I've asked him to join us; now make room for Manny, Lillian, please."

Mary's sister grudgingly moved so Manny could sit next to Mary.

"What do you do, Mister Roth?" one of them asked.

"Roth, that's a Jewish name, isn't it?"

"Our doctor is Jewish, or is he Turkish? I can never remember," another quipped.

"Like Einstein and Chaplin," Mary said.

"Well, what do you do, Mister Roth?" Mary's sister was going to do her best to discourage him.

"I'm in the dry goods business," he said.

"Don't you mean you work in a retail store and sell shoes or something?"

"Yes, that's true, among other things."

"Wait a minute! Are you Manny Roth, from Roth's department stores?" The girl at the other end was also visiting from Ontario.

"Why yes, I am. I'm flattered you've heard of me."

"You mean your father is Manny Roth, don't you?" Lillian asked.

"My father died quite a while ago, when I was thirteen. I had to start working then and well…I've never stopped."

"Mary, do you know who this is?"

Mary was quick to react. "I'm sure Mister Roth has better things to do than listen to all of you. Another dance, Mister Roth?"

He held her closer this time.

"When can I see you again, Mary?" he asked.

"I don't know, Manny. My father doesn't allow me to date men."

"You're not a child, Mary. What do you mean he doesn't allow you to date men?"

"You don't know my father. If he knew I was here, he'd kill me."

"Over my dead body," Manny assured her.

"C'mon, Mary," her sister said, taking her by the arm, pulling her toward the exit.

"Please, Mary, when can I see you again?" Manny pleaded.

"Well, I will be playing tomorrow night at the Kitz Theatre. I might have some time then, I don't know, I really must go."

Mary's jealous sister continued scolding her all the way home on the street car.

"Don't you know Father will be there tomorrow night? This is insane! Are you completely out of your mind?"

"The idea has occurred to me."

Earlier that evening Mary's father was seated at the head of the dinner table, her mother at the other end and her three sisters on either side. Dinner was always a formal occasion at the Hamptons. In fact, Mary couldn't remember a time when it was anything but. Leonard Hampton was not the kind of man who wasted his time on frivolous matters.

"God intended everything to be in its place, and that there be a place for everything. Isn't that right, Mother?"

"Yes, Leonard, a place for everything." Elli Hampton never disagreed with her husband, even those times just before he entered her. "I have my needs, Elli," he'd say.

"Well, Mary, all the time we've spent teaching you and you still can't tell the difference between a salad fork and a dinner fork, can you? This is the kind of stupidity that cannot be tolerated by decent people. You continue to shame me, don't you, Mary?"

Her father's arm reached out and pointed his index finger at the point of her shoulder. It wasn't the first poke; it was always the last. He jabbed her once, then again, hesitated, and jabbed twice more.

"What's the matter, Mary? You usually cry by now," he said.

"And there you are, Olivia. It had to be you. The one I thought might amount to something. The thought of you under the covers with that Irish loafer. I don't know if I can ever live with it. Can I, Mother? Can I?"

"No, Father; can't live with it."

"Same way I can't live with the slime our government continues to let in. Those Jews are everywhere, aren't they, Mother?"

"Yes, everywhere, Leonard."

"Damn right!"

"Oh, Daddy, you're so funny." Laura Lee, the youngest and most unaffected by her bigoted father, leapt on to his lap; none of the others had ever sat on their father's lap.

"Daddy?"

"Yes, my precious."

"Daddy, Mama keeps filling my plate. I simply can't eat as much as they do. Would you please tell Mama, Daddy, please?"

"Don't you worry, precious. If Mama does it again, she will finish your dinner for you, won't you, Mother?"

"Yes, finish it."

Leonard and Elli Hampton and their two daughters, Lillian and Mary, immigrated to Canada from England in 1921. It was a sudden departure. If the truth be told, old Leonard couldn't keep it in his pants; as an appointed magistrate and parish elder in the local Anglican Church, he held an important position; unfortunately, the position he took with one of the Sisters of Mercy had earned him a ticket out of the country. Finding his way to Vancouver, he landed employment as a diamond buyer for a national jewelry company. Leonard hated the job; he hadn't realized his employers were Jewish. He had hated Jews ever since a Jew became Prime Minister of England. No one in the family could remember a time when Leonard wasn't talking about Jews. "Those slimy bastards" was his favorite expression. His reasonable income supported the family and allowed him to purchase a nice house on a nice street on the west side, just a few blocks from the local Kitz Theatre. He watched over his family and ran the household like a judge presiding over his court, delving out the appropriate punishment for everything from untidiness to mispronunciations of the King's English. Each evening after dinner the girls, except for Laura Lee, had to recite excerpts from the Bible; each taking their turn as directed. Elli sat in her chair knitting and mumbling the last few words of each paragraph.

Mary walked flowingly across the theatre stage and sat at the piano. She wore a red velvet dress and low-heeled shoes, and her hair was up high exposing her beautiful neck. Pulling the bench to a comfortable position and with a nod to the two violinists, Mary began to play.

Manny sat motionless in the back row of the small theatre; he had never heard anyone play the piano live on stage before, and he for sure hadn't ever heard classical music. His focus was completely on Mary. He of course hadn't realized the girl he met in the bar last night possessed more than a quick wit and a pretty face. *She is an angel bringing music to the world.*

The other hundred and fifty or so were also mesmerized. Mary played with a passion beyond Manny's understanding. Tchaikovsky and Beethoven were not a part of his musical repertoire. Mary rose and stood in front of the piano. The applause rose to a higher level as she accepted the small bouquet of flowers from one of the violinists, then simply bowed, turned, and walked off giving one last wave to her adoring audience.

Later in the lobby, Manny offered his congratulations.

"That was amazing, Mary! I've never heard music like that before. It hadn't occurred to me that talent like yours even existed."

Manny cast a curious look at the man behind her. Leonard was standing there holding Mary's coat. He had been watching them from the other side of the open reception area wondering why after shaking practically all one hundred and fifty hands, she found it necessary to linger with a suspicious looking stranger.

"Oh, Father!" Mary quickly gasped for air. "Father, this is Mister Roth. Mister Roth, my father, Leonard Hampton." Leonard's angry face did nothing to shake Manny's composure.

"You must be very proud of your daughter," Manny said. "She has amazing hands." The thought of those hands finding their way into his pants quickly passed.

"Yes, very proud. How is it you know my daughter, sir?" he asked.

"Just my good fortune to have been in the neighborhood. I couldn't leave without congratulating Miss Hampton; it was really quite remarkable, don't you think?"

"I'm not in the habit of discussing my daughter's talent with strangers; come along, Mary."

"Thanks for the compliments, Mister Roth," Mary said, shaking his hand one more time, only this time leaving a note she had previously prepared in his palm.

"Good night, Mister Roth."

"Good night, Miss Hampton."

The heavy rain was coming down but no one ran inside to avoid it. The soggy procession formed a perfectly spaced line and slowly walked up the path to the front door looking like pallbearers without a casket.

Inside, Leonard waited for Mary to close the front door behind her. Slowly he brought his right arm into position; she didn't see it coming. As Mary turned to face him, Leonard's hand swept across her gentle face sending her reeling to the floor.

"I suppose you think me a fool?" he shouted.

Mary crawled to the foot of the stairs and pulled herself up by holding on to the base of the banister.

"You think I wouldn't see through your ridiculous charade? You think I don't know a kike when I see one?"

Mary sat on the floor shaking and holding her cheek as her father continued his verbal assault.

"You're a whore! In my own home, a bitch in heat, a Godless, ungrateful whore! That's what you are, and that's what you'll always be. You will never leave this house again. Do you hear me!"

Mary stood up on the first stair and glared back at him.

"Oh yes I will, Father. I won't spend another minute in Hitler's house!"

He moved toward her to deliver what was sure to be another blow to her face when Mary held a pointed finger at her father's face. He winced and fell back as Mary made a fist and waved it over his head.

"You ever touch me again and I will kill you as sure as you stand!" she said.

"Get out! Get out of my house!" he screamed.

"Oh, don't worry, Father, I'm already packed."

Manny threw the Export out and rolled up the window of the rented convertible. It was pouring now. *It's always a rainin' in Vancouver.*

Mary was dripping wet when she opened the passenger door and tossed the small suitcase in the back and got in.

"You all right?" Manny asked. She could hardly speak; the pain from her father's slap was getting worse.

"Just drive, Manny, please. Just drive," she said.

Mary sat on the bed holding her cheek in the sparsely furnished motel room. It smelled of mildew and you could hear the rain falling on the roof. Manny turned off the light to the bathroom and stood in front of her, removed his tie and unbuttoned his shirt.

It had happened so fast; what was supposed to be a one-nighter had gotten extremely complicated.

"I'll go back and give your old man what he deserves," he said.

"It's too late, Manny. It would just make things worse."

He felt sorry for her, but not sorry enough to forget about what it was he really wanted. They were cool; from the moment she first touched him, he knew. The aroma of innocence was unmistakable; he hadn't been with a virgin before and it was strangely exciting, but Manny's desire was starting to wane.

"Turn over," he said, hoping a change of position might help. "Take it in your mouth."

"I can't, I can't do that!" Mary begged.

"You will, or you'll walk home!"

Manny put both hands behind her head and forced her to take his penis into her mouth.

"Harder, suck harder!" he demanded.

She knew prostitutes did this; it was fitting she learned how. Manny's intense orgasm sent waves of pain shooting through her face.

The virgin was good; maybe I'll postpone the business deal. Maybe I should take a holiday for a couple of weeks; the investors back home will have forgotten about Vancouver by then.

"Take me with you, Manny, please! I'll do anything; please take me with you," she pleaded.

Even the horrors of last night couldn't and wouldn't be enough to make her go back to her father. Over the next two weeks the unlikely travelers made their way by car all the way to New Orleans and up the east coast before heading back to Ottawa. Mary endured everything as Manny continued to make unusual sexual demands on her, but as the days passed somehow he had become more tolerant. It was, of course, her intelligence. Although she succumbed at night, during the day she spoke to him of things he knew nothing about. He began to admire her knowledge of the arts and history, things that he might have known had he finished the sixth grade.

"Welcome back, Mister Roth." The line of admiring employees stretched all the way down the main aisle of Roth's Department Store.

Manny shook the hand of each one, stopping to give an encouraging word to everyone.

"You look wonderful today, Missus Berger," he said.

"How's the family, Irving? That boy of yours behaving himself?"

Manny spoke to all of them in their native languages. It was uncanny. He spoke six languages fluently and a couple others when he needed them. Everyone spoke a different language back in Grand Prairie. Everyone was an immigrant from somewhere.

"If you were going to sell something to someone, you better be able to sell it in their own language." It was his mother of course; she never said the same thing twice in the same language.

Except for Manny's little secret, it was business as usual. Mary was holed up in a small broken-down motel on the outskirts of town. She'd been there two weeks before Manny showed up to restock the icebox.

"How long do you expect me to live like this?" she asked. "I don't see you for weeks; there's nothing to do but listen to this old radio."

"Look, Mary, I will try to find you something more comfortable, I promise."

"But what about us?" she shouted.

"I told you this from the start; I'd be ruined if anyone knew about you!"

"You mean your shiksa, right?"

"If you're going to stay, you can't be seen; it's as simple as that. Now stop all this and come here."

A year passed and with each day Manny became more nervous about Mary. It was true, he would be ruined if anyone found out about his Christian whore. It wouldn't matter if Manny Roth's name was on every charity foundation roster in eastern Canada. No one would care that Roth's department stores provided jobs to desperate new immigrants. If anyone from the synagogue or any of his Jewish investors knew that he kept a shiksa in a beaten-down old house five miles out of town, Manny Roth and Roth's department stores would no longer exist.

Nineteen thirty-nine—war had broken out in Europe. As a loyal member of the Commonwealth, Canada was called upon to fight the Nazis.

Manny leaned on his desk, covered his face and thought about his father. He too would become a soldier fighting on the battlefield for a dream come true. Manny, just like his father, would learn to kill an enemy and fight to the end for freedom and justice. This was his chance to be the man his father always wanted him to be.

"What do you mean, you're going to enlist? What about me?" Mary shouted.

"I'm sorry, Mary, but duty calls and I must fight. I've decided, and that's that."

"That's that, is it?" she said. "Well, who's going to help me with the baby? Answer me that, mister that's that?"

"You're pregnant?" Manny's face reddened.

"Yes, I'm pregnant! Now, what are you going to do?"

Mary had little hope that the blessed event meant anything more than an inconvenience to him. Without saying a word, Manny just turned and walked out the door. Mary followed behind grabbing his arm and spinning him around.

"If you go now, everyone will know about your shiksa whore; do you hear me? Everyone!"

"Sorry, Mister Roth, you're just too short. Regulations are regulations. There is nothing I can do. Please, step aside. Next!"

Manny walked slowly out of the recruiting station and got in his new Buick and drove away. He must have driven a hundred miles before stopping on the roadside, finally pulling over to find a place to relieve himself. It was then he became aware how far he had gone. It was close to ten p.m. when he knocked on Mary's door.

"They don't want me, Mary. I'm too damn short!" he said.

She held him that night; there were no demands, just the two of them holding each other like people do when they're in love. For the first time in a year Mary felt there was hope, hope for a life that could be shared with another; a house, a home and a family.

"How does the name Elizabeth sound?" she asked. Manny didn't answer; he had fallen asleep in her arms and stayed that way until morning.

Although they remained out of sight, Mary and Manny began to spend more and more time together, taking walks in the countryside, holding hands and talking about the future.

"It won't always be like this, Mary, I promise," he said.

Elizabeth Anne Roth was born April 9, 1940. It was a hard delivery, made harder by Manny's absence. While Mary labored for fifteen hours, Manny was accepting a plaque as Ottawa's favorite son in front of the Manny Roth Orphanage.

As much as he wanted to change things for Mary, he couldn't escape the world he had made for himself. He soon became more and more irritable and more distant to her.

Ten months later, the announcement of another pregnancy was more than Manny could stand.

"You're what! Oh, this is great, just what I needed. Listen, Mary, I know this guy, he can help us get out of this."

"Do you mean an abortion?" she asked.

"Well, what did you think I meant?"

"Never! Never in a million years! We were going to be a family! We were happy. You won't do this to me! Do you understand! You won't do this to me!"

He was caught living in his own nightmare. He had become the captive and there was nothing he could do. The war was still going badly; the allies were getting pummeled in North Africa and Manny couldn't escape thinking he had betrayed his country as well as his father. He started spending less time in the office, choosing to sleep away the mornings instead.

His absence at temple started the rumors; above all else, it was his religious associations that had kept Manny Roth on top. Without them there wouldn't be a Roth's Department Store or a Manny Roth Orphanage.

Five more years and Roth was barely hanging on. Mary tried her best to cheer him up but nothing had worked so far.

"The war will be over soon, Manny. Business is bound to pick up," she told him.

"I guess so," he said. "I really don't care, anymore."

Elizabeth, now five, and Aaron, four, did little to cheer him up. His feelings of despair were deepening and his headaches made it impossible for him to function. Mary even tried to be more passionate in bed but even there she was unable to make a difference.

Nineteen forty-five; the war ended in victory for the Allies. Manny and Mary drove to Buffalo and stayed in a fancy hotel, ate an excellent dinner and even made love before returning the next day. It was a day that would change their lives forever. The rumors had stopped; they weren't rumors any longer.

"Manny, I don't think there's a right way of saying this." Al Bloom really didn't care how he said it. "The board of governors has requested you resign from the synagogue."

Harold Wine cared even less.

"Manny, we feel it would be better to change the name from the Manny Roth Orphanage to the Ottawa Home for Children; you understand?"

"Manny, we have no choice; the loan must be paid off by the end of the month; no hard feelings."

Suddenly Manny's empire was crumbling and no one would tell him why until that day in the deli.

"I hear he's got her hidden away in an old, rundown house outside of town. What have you heard?"

"Yes, I heard the same, and those two bastard children, what a disgrace."

Manny paid the bill and left the small deli restaurant. The humiliation he felt after hearing the two yentas drove him even deeper into depression. He could hardly sign his name without shaking as the two lawyers helped to steady his arm. He had sold Roth's to a guy named Weis for a fraction of its value. No one would have paid more, not to a whoremonger like Manny Roth.

"I think I can get you maybe fifteen cents on the dollar for the inventory, but the equity after debt on the real estate, well, it's not going to be much. Prices have really dropped. You understand," they said.

It was all over town; Manny Roth had been keeping a shiksa whore for six years while he was president of the synagogue. That evening Manny told the children to "scat" and proceeded to berate Mary like he hadn't done in years. He swore at her and called her every name he could think of until finally forcing her to the floor and practically raping her. Without even looking back, Manny left the house, never to return.

He left her some money, at least enough to care for her and the children for awhile. Still too proud, Mary would never return to her father's house. With her fate uncertain, Mary was more alone than ever before.

Mary lay half asleep on the tear-drenched bed, shaking and delirious from fever. The ceiling and walls were closing in on her. She could see the grotesque and deformed images of her father's and sisters' faces staring at her; blood dripped from their eyes as they called her a whore. The pain in her chest and stomach was replaced with fear and panic as water gushed from inside her. She tried screaming for help but nothing came out. Suddenly the door to her bedroom opened. Grace Weeks, a single mother and Mary's only friend, came rushing in.

"Mary! Mary! Let me help you."

"How did you know?" Mary whispered.

"How did I know? I heard you screaming for me. I heard you calling my name! It was bouncing off the walls in my basement."

"But, Grace, you live two blocks away."

It was July 13, 1946.

Chapter Seven

"Manny?"

"Seth!"

"Yep, it's me. Guess you didn't think you'd hear from me again, did ya, cowboy? I heard ya had some trouble and well, it's a different world now; know what I mean?"

"Seth, Seth, I can't believe it's you! Where are you? Are you here?"

"Sure am; wanna meet?"

"Sure do."

"See you at Randy's in an hour."

"Randy's!"

"She won't be back for hours; I'd come to see you but I can't leave. Listen, if you don't want to, I understand. I just thought I could help."

Manny needed help, and fast.

They sat and talked over the good old days for an hour before Manny got around to blaming his failing business and reputation on a bitter shiksa he picked up in a bar in Vancouver. Seth was shocked beyond belief.

"Are you telling me you kidnapped a young, talented musician, took her away from her family and kept her in obscurity for six years, then had three bastard children with her and now you've abandoned her to fend for herself? Are you completely out of your fucking mind?"

Seth went crazy; he was visibly shaken from the horror of it. "You insane bastard!" he said. "How could you do such a horrible thing? You sick son of a bitch. I can't believe a person could do that to another person. I can't look at you." Seth had never shown this side of himself. His good nature and handsome face was all Manny ever saw until now. "You better do right by her, Manny, or if there is a God, he shall surely strike you down."

"Ya, well, I couldn't believe my best friend would ever betray me, either."

"Look, buster, for your information, I never did anything with Randy. She begged me not to tell you. She only wanted to save you and her from the shame and embarrassment of being your Jewish whore. She knew she'd never fit in with your crowd. She was doing you a favor, you schmuck."

"I loved her," Manny said.

"That's even sicker! What you've done to Mary, you would have done to Randy."

Seth stood over him, his expression more of pity now.

"Do right by her, Manny, or so help me God, you will answer for it." Seth turned away and walked down the corridor towards Randy's bedroom.

Manny's world had come crushing in; he became consumed by guilt, and after confessing to Bessy, even his loving mother was horrified.

"I have three grandchildren! And you don't even tell your own mother?" Bessy slapped the top of Manny's bald head. "This is a shame no mother should have to bear."

The fact that Mary wasn't Jewish was far less tragic than the shame Bessy felt.

"Whatever were you thinking?" she asked. Bessy spoke in Yiddish; there were words in Yiddish that better described her feeling for what her son had done.

"You have shamed me, your sister and your dead father."

Bessy, suddenly reminded of how her husband had treated Manny as a child, soon changed her feelings of anger to those of pity. As she looked down on her weeping son, she knew it would take her loving heart and her courage to survive that would give her the strength to endure even this.

"He was a hard man, your father," she said. "But, Manny, I don't care how you do it, you will make things right—shiksa or no shiksa, do you hear me, Manny? You will go to her and her family and beg them to forgive you. Do you understand me?"

Elli Hampton, the once quiet and obedient wife, had taken the old bull by the horns so to speak. She found out the whereabouts of her daughter, called her on the phone and convinced her to bring her grandchildren home.

They sat across the kitchen table from each other; nine-month-old Nathan lay in Mary's arms, his mouth tight to her breast. The telephone rang but neither of them seemed startled. They knew who it was; this would make the third call this week.

"It's Manny," her mother said. "He wants to talk to you." Mary shook her head and tried to pacify baby Nathan.

"I'm sorry, Manny. She won't speak to you."

"Could I at least speak to Elizabeth or Aaron?"

"I'm sorry, they're out right now. Listen to me, Manny. If giving the dubious name of Roth to my daughter is more than you can bear, I doubt anything you could say will make a difference. Goodbye, Manny."

Mary still refused to sit down to dinner with her father, choosing to have her meals in the kitchen with her mother. Her mother had changed; she was no longer willing to listen to Leonard's opinions or tolerate his outspoken hatred for Jews. Her daughter had suffered more than any young woman should have and she made no bones about whom she blamed.

"You say one more thing about Jews or about Manny, and I will see you dead in your bed! Is that clear, Leonard?"

"Yes, Mother, very clear."

In fact, Leonard hadn't said a negative thing to Mary or anyone else since she moved in with them. He did his best to avoid her and only smiled and said "good morning" once or twice when their paths did cross. It wasn't too long before Mary's hatred for her father began to fade. She would never completely forget his abuse but at least he was making an effort with her children.

Leonard didn't agree that it was he who drove his daughter into the arms of the little, "slimy bastard," but he truly believed that her punishment for running away was indeed excessive. He never spoke to Mary in the normal way again, but when he was with the grandchildren his angry disposition took on a dramatic metamorphosis. They called him Gramps, and although he never told them he loved them, the children were fascinated and delighted to sit on Gramp's knee and listen to stories about a group of enchanted monkeys named Bimbo, Jackoh and Little Mary, and their archrival orangutan, an impish mischief-maker who loved making life difficult as they searched for adventure in a fantasy jungle.

It had been almost two years since the last phone call to Mary. Manny was a beaten man; thirty-three years old and he was already bearing crosses most men spend a lifetime acquiring. It wasn't anything he said exactly that made her agree to his offer of marriage. The flowers and the ring helped, but she knew it wouldn't be a marriage based on love. At least the children wouldn't have to spend their lives thinking they were bastards.

With what little money he had left, Manny bought a nice house in a good neighborhood on the west side. Both Elizabeth and Aaron were doing well in school and Manny was getting started again with his new agency in the garment district. Mary stayed home and looked after young Nathan, no easy task considering baby Nathan was prone to fits of anger and cried from morning to night. Only Bessy could get him to stop.

"This child needs a lot of attention, Mary," she said. "He doesn't like being left alone."

Bessy said a lot of things to Mary, none of which did little to help ease the tension between them.

"I should think you would want to give these children a chance for happiness. You leave them Godless, and who will bless them? You? They are the great-grandchildren of Rabbi Emanuel Cohen! They need to honor his name. You must convert!"

She had taken Manny as her husband and it was now imperative she take his religion as well. She was never going to have a loving mother-in-law; in fact, they would never care for each other, but Mary believed Bessy was right. The children's name was Roth and there was no doubt she should convert, because it would be easier in the long run. Manny reluctantly agreed and found a Reform rabbi who, although hesitant to perform the conversion and the subsequent marriage ceremony, did so on the promise of generous support to the construction of a new synagogue, something about which Manny knew all too well. Even Leonard agreed it was the right thing to do—a huge step for a man who hated Jews as much as he did.

Manny spent his days at the office doing what he did best, selling. He still had contacts in the east, and with the same determination he had always shown, he began building another empire. He had secured agency agreements with ladies clothing manufactures and began traveling across the western provinces selling coats and dresses. Soon he was representing the largest firms in the country, and within two years he was traveling coast to coast. This of course kept him away from home more than six months each year.

As the days and weeks passed, Mary had little else to do except sit around with Nathan and wait until her other children got home from school. Liz and Aaron were always at school or at their friends. Finally Mary asked her next-door neighbor to take Nathan for the day, as his constant crying kept her up all night and she needed to sleep. If she slept she wouldn't have to think about the night Nathan was conceived. It was then that Mary began her descent into darkness, a darkness where dreams became reality and where reality was loathsome and filled with self-hatred.

"Mary, I'm home!" Manny called from the bottom of the stairs. *Two months away and not even a hello.* "Mary?" he called again, and still nothing.

Manny entered the upstairs bedroom and saw Mary lying in bed; the covers were pulled up over her head and she was facing away from him.

"Mary, are you awake? I'm home; are you sick?" He walked to the other side of the bed but Mary quickly turned away. "Mary, for goodness sakes, what's going on?"

Manny slowly pulled the sheets down and uncovered her as he screamed in horror.

"What have you done? Who did this to you? Where are the children? My God, this can't be happening!" Manny stared in disbelief; Mary's face was covered with small bandages that barely held the blood from dripping down her nose and cheeks. Her hair was thick with blood; it fell over her forehead, covering a gaping hole in the center just below her hairline.

"I couldn't stop," she said, moaning. "They came out of me; I couldn't stop them."

After waiting all night, Manny was finally able to speak to the attending doctor.

"Your wife has suffered a mental breakdown, Mister Roth, and, well, she says she saw things in her face and basically started to remove them with, uh, scissors and a nail file."

The doctor told Manny that not only had Mary done this out of a psychotic compulsion, but the deep cuts had become infected. They would do what they could, but Mary's face would be a mass of scars for the rest of her life. She was in the hospital for a month and a half before the doctors let her go home.

"You're going to need to see a psychiatrist, Missus Roth," they said. "And it's going to take a long time."

It did take a long time; it would be five years before Mary was able to leave the house again.

Lillian Hampton laid the tray of tea and toast on Mary's bedside table and wiped the drops of perspiration from her sister's forehead, being careful of course not to touch the bandages.

"Good morning, dear sister," she said. "How are we feeling this wonderful morning?" Mary didn't answer. "Now, is there anything else I can bring you, my dear, before…"

"Thank you, Lil. I'm sure there are many other things you'd rather be doing."

"Now, now; let's not start that again," she said.

Lillian was still Lillian Hampton, and though she had succeeded in bedding several suitors, none of them had ever popped the question. Having spent the last five years traveling around the world, she thought it would do her good to settle down and help with the children and her tragically ill sister; it was the least she could do.

It might not have been so bad if she could get that Nathan to shut up for more than five minutes.

"Have you seen my husband? I need to speak to him," Mary said.

"I saw him early this morning, dear, but I think he's gone to see your neighbor —you know, the man he goes to lodge with."

"I suppose you fixed his breakfast before he left?"

"And the children's. Honestly, that Nathan, I'm sure he's going to be an opera singer one day, with those lungs. Mary? I've asked some friends over for cards this afternoon, I hope you don't mind."

"Why should I mind? It's only my house."

"Good, I knew you would understand. I'll make sure no one bothers you; just ring if you need anything."

Mary's deep frown went unnoticed by her doting sister. Each day she grew more and more suspicious of her.

The stale air lingered in the dimly-lit room; perspiration from their bodies and the too soft mattress made it impossible to gain adequate leverage. The two of them struggled for a quick end to their betrayal.

Lillian pulled the covers up under her arms, lit a cigarette and appeared unaffected by Manny's sudden eagerness to depart.

"I can't say that was the best time I've spent between the sheets," she said.

"What's that supposed to mean?"

"Well, you don't exactly make a girl swoon, do you now, brother-in-law?" Her mocking tone didn't go over well.

"You're not the best I've ever had, either."

"Is that so? Well, at least my poor sister doesn't have to endure you."

"You bitch!" Manny's face began to redden. "You're the cause of this. You come into our home, pretend to care about your sister and end up screwing her husband and grabbing onto everything that isn't nailed down. In my books that makes you a cheap whore, and I regret ever letting you in." Manny finished dressing and glared at her. "I want you out of this house by the time I get back." He closed the door and walked downstairs, picking up the mail on his way out.

An hour later Manny slumped in his office chair; his eyes were closed and an arm dangled over the side holding an opened letter. He had read it over and over again; each time the words fell over him like a blanket of nails.

> *Dear Manny*
>
> *We are writing you in hopes that you will join us in celebrating our wedding. You are our dearest friend. And though it's been a long time, our love has lasted through the worst of times. Please come and be our best man. We miss you and look forward to starting over.*
>
> *Mary will love California.*
>
> *All our love*
>
> *Randy and Seth*

Seth held her as Randy wept; her tears mingled with his own as the two of them stood trembling with anticipation.

"There aren't enough tears in the ocean that will change my mind," he whispered. "I love you and I will always love you."

The rabbi placed his hands on their shoulders.

"Dear God, by joining these wonderful people in the sanctity of marriage You have proven Your love for them. Oh, Lord, we thank Thee for all our blessings. We thank Thee for Your mercy and Your gift of love. Oh, Lord, watch over Randy and Seth and grant them the sight to see Your love and to know the power of it."

The rabbi raised his arms and reached out over the congregation.

"May the Lord bless you and keep you and give you peace. Amen."

Placing the paper bag on the ground, the rabbi gave Seth his permission to "break the glass and seal your love forever." Seth raised his foot and smashed the glass.

"Mazel tov!" Everyone shouted the cheer of congratulations.

There wasn't a dry eye among the three hundred invited guests. Seth and Randy Penner moved back up the aisle hand in hand, waving at all who cheered them. The happiness and tears of joy on their faces would have a lasting impression, and in spite of all that had happened, no one doubted that Randy and Seth Penner would live happily ever after.

Outside on the temple stairs, Randy embraced the silver haired Russian.

"Oh, Sal, was there anything, anything at all?"

Sal Gold smiled sadly. "I'm sorry, my dear, not a word."

Manny sat motionless as the aircraft struggled for altitude. The migraine had worn him out; with his face red and his eyes swollen and shut, he struggled with his deepest fears. At first there was pain and sorrow, now only anger and hatred remained. *If it weren't for her and her bastard children none of this would have happened to me. God damn them all.*

Chapter Eight

"Oooooh! That's cold, Momma!" Four-year-old Nathan shivered and shook as Mary pulled the damp canvas life preserver over his pudgy body. Manny stood above them looking down from the wharf above, his hands on the wooden railing.

"Just throw the sissy in...he'll swim; won't you, Nathan?"

"Momma! Please, Momma, don't throw me in."

Mary held him close to her; the shoreline was jagged and slippery. She took him swimming every day after dinner, letting him paddle around in the safe waters between the dock and the rocky shore. She felt safer with her parents than with Manny; Nathan was also safer here. Leonard had come out of retirement and accepted a position in the new municipality of Sechelt, about sixty miles north by ferry from Vancouver. They sold the old house and Elli and Leonard took up residence in a quaint waterfront home about an hour's drive from where he worked.

Mary and the children made the five-hour journey over gravel roads that wouldn't be paved for ten more years. They came on the odd weekend and over the summer holidays until Nathan was six and ready for school. Mary came to share her misery with her mother. Lizzy and Aaron came to do what ten- and eleven-year-old kids do, swim and play in the sun. Manny came to see Leonard. In spite of everything that had happened, Leonard and Manny got along better than anyone ever expected. Over the past five years they built a second house on the property; one that could house the other daughter's family, and a boat on which the two of them spent day after day fishing for salmon along British Columbia's Pacific coastline.

One Sunday morning the friendship came to an abrupt end. Leonard stood on the dock as Manny tied off the lines.

"How many times have I told you not to exceed the posted speed in the harbor?" he shouted. Leonard didn't wait for Manny to answer; he just handed him the citation for speeding. They never spoke again.

Later that year Manny moved the family into a large Tudor house he purchased off a foreclosure. It included the furniture and a white baby grand that sat predominantly in front of the large bay window. Mary was thrilled; she played for hours every day, sometimes forgetting all about four-year-old Nathan who sat quietly beneath the blue velvet-covered bench.

She began each session with Brahms. The deep and flowing melodies of the master echoed throughout the large house. Nathan was content and comforted by them. Next it was Beethoven, more intense now. Mary always had difficulty with Beethoven; it made her lose concentration as the difficult changes took her in and out of the moment, sometimes resulting in her banging the keys in frustration.

"Are you mad at me, Momma?" Nathan asked.

Mary didn't answer; she sat hunched over with her eyes closed, exhausted from the power of the concerto.

"Momma, are you sad?"

Little Nathan stood next to her patting her shoulder. She looked at him but still said nothing; Mary had a way of looking right through people, not even seeing them.

Nathan felt safe under the piano bench, at least for a while anyway. He'd run upstairs and hide under his bed or in a closet when Manny came home. He couldn't bear hearing his mother cry; she always cried when Daddy came home.

In the early evening less than a year later, Manny stood with his hands on his hips glaring at her from the other side of the piano.

"Stop that racket! Can't you, for Christ's sake, make me some dinner? My God, woman, can't you see I'm tired!" he shouted. "By the way, I've sold the house. We have to be out by the end of the month."

For a few thousand dollars profit, the large Tudor home was history, grand piano and all. Manny bought a much smaller house in a new subdivision, but, to his surprise, no one was pleased, especially Aaron, who now had to share a bedroom with his disgusting little brother. He'd resented Nathan ever since he was introduced to him. "They brought the little shit home on my birthday," he said to his sister. "That screaming brat was the only present I got."

For anyone looking in it appeared normal enough, the five members of the Roth family having dinner together at home. No one would suspect that underneath the façade each member harbored his or her own growing resentment of each other.

"Do we have to hear him eat in stereo?" Aaron whispered in Nathan's ear.

"Aaron! That's not nice," Nathan said.

Manny glared at Nathan but continued chewing loudly. Aaron leaned to his right and whispered into his ten-year-old brother's ear once more.

"You know what really makes me sick? Eating my dinner while sitting next to a piece of dreck like you."

Nathan flicked the back of his hand at Aaron's arm, barely touching him, but it gave Aaron the perfect opportunity to strike back.

"Owe!" Nathan screamed.

"Nathan!" Manny shouted.

"But he called me a piece of dreck."

"Oh, sure I did. I told you he was crazy, Father."

"But he started it."

"Nathan! Shut up and go to your room. You're always doing this."

"But!"

"Don't you dare talk back to me! Get out of my sight! And don't come back until you know how to act like a human being."

Nathan seldom finished his dinner before being sent to his room for something his brother had done. Aaron could make it happen any time he felt the urge; there was no defense against him. Each day Nathan became more and more terrified of his brother; at night, Aaron laughed himself to sleep, tormenting him with stories of the bogeyman.

"He's coming to get you, Nathan," he said, "and there's nothing you can do about it. He always comes when you're asleep."

Each night Nathan waited in darkness until Mary was able to avoid Manny and bring him something to eat.

"You all right, Nathan?" she asked.

"Uh hu." Mary sat next to him drying his tears with a kitchen towel.

"It's going to be all right, Nathan. He's leaving tomorrow; he won't be back for a month or two."

"Good! I hate him. I wish you had married someone else."

After a kiss on his cheek, Mary quietly closed the bedroom door behind her.

It took only a moment before Nathan's tears resumed their constant flow. He lay on his small bed staring up at the ceiling. The tear-soaked pillow under his head caused him to shiver and shake. The same questions he asked every night began to fill his thoughts.

Why doesn't anyone love me? Why couldn't I have a father like the other kids? I see the neighbors' children playing in their backyards jumping and wrestling with their dads. Why does my father hate me so much? Why doesn't my sister ever talk to me? Why won't my mother help me? Oh, God, please help me. Help me be a good boy so they will like me again. Why did you make my mother ugly? Was she bad? Please help my mother. Hopelessness and despair were his covers; peace and freedom was his destiny.

Billy Bickerton lived across the lane. Like most kids in the neighborhood, he took great pleasure in tormenting Nathan.

"Your mother is so ugly, she must eat frogs," he said laughingly. "Does your mother eat oats, like the other horses?" Billy laughed even harder.

"Does your mother eat snakes? Is that why she's soooooo ugly?"

Nathan had had enough; his anger now raging inside him. He punched Billy Bickerton as hard as he had ever punched anything. The neighborhood bully screamed and went down like a rock. A minute latter Misses Bickerton came running into the yard and grabbed him.

"You little bastard!" she screamed, and slapped Nathan across his face, sending him crying and running into the house.

"What happened?" Mary asked, trying to console him.

"It was Mrs. Bickerton; she slapped me."

"She what! We'll see about this."

Mary became hysterical. She'd been baking cookies and still held the rolling pin as she stormed out the back door and down the steps and across the lane to the Bickertons' house. She banged on the kitchen door.

"Come out, you bitch! You touch my son again and I'll kill you!"

Mrs. Bickerton crouched beneath the kitchen counter; there was no way she was going to open the door for that crazy Roth woman. *God, what if her face is contagious?*

Nathan loved the neighborhood drive-ins. The White Spot was his favorite; not having to sit at the dining room table with the usual terror was as good as it got.

"I'll have chicken pickens and a Coke, Mom."

"And I'll have the same. Thank you."

"Thank you, ma'am," said the red-headed carhop.

Nathan thought he was very polite, but as the green Buick pulled into the space next to them, he knew the people in it wouldn't be.

"Look, Mom! Look at the monster!" the two freckle-faced teenagers shouted from the back seat.

Nathan saw the two boys in the Buick starring and pointing at Mary. Mary also heard it but, as usual, refused to look or say anything. No one in the family ever said anything about Mary's face. Nathan just sat there glaring back at them. *God will surely strike you down for being so cruel.* It was always the same unexplainable feeling he got whenever he was out with his mother; someone was sure to stare and gasp. He hated them all. *Someday they will be punished.* Of this he was certain.

It was 1958 and Nathan wasn't the only one living in fear. The whole world was afraid, especially in North America where people were building bomb shelters in their basements. The television networks were constantly reminding people of the horrors and atrocities of WWII. Films and news footage of Hiroshima and Nagasaki were televised everyday. The atomic bomb and the future of all humanity depended on who had more nuclear bombs, the Americans or the Communists.

Nathan pulled the covers over his head; he knew it was a dream, but the light he saw was still burning inside his head. His trembling body was soaked in perspiration as the images gradually faded from his mind. The recurring dream had woken him almost every night for months. The world was burning, aglow with radiation from a thousand nuclear explosions. He saw the faces of children crying and heard their screams as they ran from the fire. He had fallen on molten flesh and felt the flames on his body. The world was crumbling under him; desperately, he reached out and tried to cover the light burning from above.

Manny was traveling more than ever. He had seized an opportunity to start his own manufacturing business making ladies fir-trimmed coats and knitted suits; but even rapid success did nothing to change his attitude towards Mary or the children. He refused to buy anything for the house, though it was desperately in need of repairs. "If you want something, get a job," he said. It would be a huge step, but with a renewed spirit Mary did get a job. Mary had an uncanny talent for typing and after a little practice became even more confident; it was only a few months before she became indispensable.

"Thank God for you, Mary. I don't know what I did before you got here." The small office was perfect, not a lot of people, just her and her boss. Leo Marks was the president of the western chapter of the Zionist Organization of Canada and a kind and gentle man who took to Mary right off. Of course it was her incredible speed on the typewriter that made her a great employee, but soon a friendship was formed, allowing them to share their life's experiences, telling each other things they told no one else.

Leo had been a pilot during Israel's war of independence and in spite of witnessing the horror of it, remained serene, treating Mary with the utmost respect and courtesy. *What a father he would have made for Nathan.* She pondered the idea as if it was somehow possible, like a fairytale.

"This is my son Nathan," Mary said. "Say hello to Mister Marks, Nathan."

"Call me Leo. Your mother tells me you like baseball, eh, Nathan?"

"I sure do, Mister Marks…I mean, Leo."

"You know they play a lot of baseball at Camp Zion. You know, Mary, Nathan could go to camp this summer for half the price. How does that sound, young Nathan?"

"It sounds wonderful! Will it be OK, Mom? I mean, you know."

"Don't worry, Nathan," she said. "I will make it OK."

Camp Zion was located on the shores of Lake Kalamalka in the Okanogan Valley, commonly known as the Canadian desert. The twenty acres had been purchased by the Zionist organization, and for eight glorious weeks in the summer, two hundred Jewish children, ages twelve to fifteen, enjoyed a summer camp atmosphere with all the swimming, canoeing and numerous other activities of a regular camp. But unknown to many, the camp was really the preliminary training ground for those children who showed the first signs of becoming a leader in the Zionist movement.

Leo Marks, now forty-two, was one of the first to come back to Canada after fighting for Israel's independence. Leo accepted the position as the western president with the unwritten mandate to establish Camp Zion as the premier Zionist camp in the country. He was extremely pleased when Mary agreed to send Nathan.

"He doesn't really know anything about being Jewish, Leo. Do you think he'll be OK? I mean, do you think he'll fit in?"

"Don't worry, Mary," he said. "I'll be there to watch over him."

The first two weeks were very difficult for Nathan; though Mary had converted to Judaism, Nathan knew nothing about being a Jew other than some children at school seemed to hate them. There was never a tree, but Mary left presents at the end of his bed on every Christmas morning—so he knew about Christ. Camp Zion was Nathan's first experience with anything to do with what it meant to be Jewish. Manny never took the children to temple and any religious feelings he had had as a child were long forgotten.

Friday nights at camp were the best. The Sabbath was a celebration, and everyone at camp put on their best blue pants and best white shirt and rejoiced as if God himself was joining in the fun.

Nathan sat at his cabin table in the chadar and recited the Hebrew blessing before eating.

Baruch atah adenoy elohanew melech hoalom hamotzie lechem meana oritz. Amen.

Leo Marks sat at the center of the head table; his six counselors sat on either side keeping a watchful eye on their respective tables. Each counselor was responsible for his own cabin of twelve kids who, to say the least, were far more interested in swimming and fishing than learning over and over again the principals and practices of Judaism. Nathan, however, couldn't get enough. He quickly identified with the plight and history of the Jewish people. *All must suffer if we are to know what it is to be a Jew.* He loved the language and picked up Hebrew words and phrases far easier that he should have. He was fascinated with the possibility that God might actually exist. Up to that point Nathan's happiness had been in the hands of those who despised him. Now he began to believe that it was God who determined his destiny and not his father. Unfortunately, getting along with the other kids was harder than he had hoped. They seemed uncomfortable around him; one boy especially couldn't speak to him without calling him "Christian" or "half-breed." Nathan ignored them for the most part; he was content in the company of the *rosh* counselor and the other older counselors.

Sechut was his favorite time of all. Leo and maybe six or seven others, mostly counselors, sat together on the rocks overlooking the pastel-colored lake.

"They thought we were a commercial airliner, just coming in for a landing." Leo laughed again. "Otherwise, why would we have had all our running lights on?"

Leo finished telling one of his best stories about the war in Israel. Nathan had heard it twice before, but he didn't mind. He loved to listen to Leo talk about his exploits as a pilot and soldier fighting for his beloved country. He didn't know such things happened to people until now. His whole world up to then had been trying to avoid his brother and sister. He didn't have to avoid his father; Manny was better at it than he.

By the end of the summer Nathan Roth was a Jew, not just in name but also in his mind and in his soul. A year later and another summer under his belt, Nathan no longer lay in bed crying himself to sleep. After another boring day at school, and in Nathan's mind a complete waste of time, he hopped a bus to his mother's office where ZOC held meetings on the top floor. Sometimes visiting rabbis would discuss religious issues and other times leading Zionists spoke of the continuing crisis in Israel.

Dinner table conversations at home were much different now. Nathan didn't sit next to his brother anymore. Now that Liz was married and gone, Aaron couldn't whisper in her ear.

"*Tainlee avockashaw lechem*, Aaron?" he said, asking in Hebrew for his brother to pass the bread.

"For God's sake! Do we have to listen to this every day?" Aaron's cutting remark brought no response from his twelve-year-old sibling.

"It's about time we practice our religion, don't you think, Father?"

Manny just sat there shaking his head and thinking what a mistake his stupid wife had made.

"Father, I think it's time to talk about my bar mitzvah, don't you? I was speaking to Leo and he thinks the best place for me is the Talmud Torah."

Manny's face began to redden as he stared at Mary.

"What do you think, Father?" Nathan asked.

"The Talmud Torah is expensive," he replied. "Who do you think is going to pay for it? You?"

"But, Father, this is important."

"Go to your room, Nathan, and don't..."

"I will not!" Nathan shouted.

"You will or..."

"Or what, Father, you gonna hit me?"

Oddly enough, Manny had never hit any of the children; in spite of all his torments, they didn't have to relive what he had lived. Nathan calmly stood and walked out of the room, followed by Aaron a minute later.

"You're in real trouble now, shithead," Aaron said.

Nathan rose from the bed and stood directly in front of his older brother.

"Get out of my room, Aaron," he said.

"Or what, shithead?"

"Get out of my room, Aaron."

Aaron stood fast. Nathan's right hand closed to a fist and caught his brother with a straight punch to the jaw, knocking him to the ground.

"What the hell have you done now, Nathan?" Manny shouted.

"It's OK, Dad, I'm fine," Aaron said, as he suddenly felt inexplicably proud of his little brother. The days of Aaron abusing Nathan were over.

Nathan glared with disgust at his father before closing his bedroom door.

Nathan lay on his bed and thought about the future. *If not the Talmud Torah, then where? Who will teach me? There must be someone who could prepare me for my bar mitzvah. It is already November; I'll be thirteen in July. What most Jewish children learn in six or seven years, I have to learn in less than six months, but who will teach me?* The answer came sooner than he could have imagined.

"My name is Cantor Green," he said. "We will start with ancient Hebrew."

Nathan could hardly believe his luck. Cantor Green had given a talk at one of the ZOC meetings and Leo had introduced him. He was fifty, tall, and wore a short Vandyke.

It wasn't long before Cantor Green began to suspect that his newest student was somehow different than most children his age. He couldn't put his finger on it, but he saw something that reminded him of how he felt when he was a child. The fact that Nathan had no religious training at all was a challenge he accepted. He knew Nathan's desire to learn would truly set him apart.

Every other day for the next six months, Nathan and Cantor Green met at the ZOC. Nathan read from the Torah while the cantor listened. He hadn't needed to correct his most enthusiastic student in weeks. There was a basic routine: history and the Bible, then Hebrew and music. It was more than apparent that Nathan didn't share the cantor's love for ancient history; he was far more interested in the language than the stories in the Bible.

"Cantor?" Nathan asked. "Don't you think God would be completely bored listening to stories he's heard every day for five thousand years?"

"OK, Nathan, music it is. Close the book; we'll start with the third modulation."

It was the music that took him to the next level of understanding. The ancient melodies allowed him to express the words as he felt they were meant to be expressed.

"By the way, Cantor..."

"What is it now, Nathan?"

"Has it occurred to you that the Bible teaches us what was, instead of what is?"

The cantor had grown accustomed to Nathan's curious questions.

"Nothing has changed, Nathan," he said. "People are still in need of guidance."

"But, Cantor, if you wanted to make things better, surely you can't do that it in the past, can you? I mean, the Bible is all about the past. I believe God still operates today. Don't you, Cantor?"

"Yes, Nathan. Now, let's concentrate on your *maftir*."

His title was Cantor Green, but to the congregation in the small orthodox synagogue he was Rabbi Green. The old temple was located ninety miles south of Vancouver, in the small boarder town of Bellingham, Washington. It would be there where Nathan made his leap to manhood.

Though it was an orthodox synagogue, Cantor Green was a Conservative rabbi. Women and men could sit together in a Conservative synagogue. The Roth family, looking conspicuously uncomfortable, took up the first row behind the canopy. Aaron sat next to his father, and then Mary. Lizzy and her new husband sat next to Bessy and her newest and oldest husband yet. They had made the journey from Calgary as part of their honeymoon.

Nathan and Rabbi Green entered from the door next to the pulpit and took their seats against the wall and under the Ark. Moments later Nathan stood and walked around and up the stairs to the centered, canopied pulpit, faced the Ark and thanked the two elders who unrolled the old Torah scroll in front of him. He held the prayer shawl in his hand and touched the *tzitzi* to the scroll and kissed them.

For six months Nathan had been obsessed with learning and understanding everything about his religion. It wasn't enough to simply learn how to read Hebrew, he had to know what the words meant. The hours he spent in his room where he once laid crying night after night had been his sanctuary, sometimes studying through the night. Neither his angry father nor his malevolent brother could distract him.

Nathan placed his hands on the gold handles of the Torah and felt a surge of energy rush up his arms and into his chest.

Outside, white clouds silently raced by the synagogue's stained-glass windows then disappeared into the late summer sun.

The first few words were soft and barely audible.

"*Tafilo lahavakook hanovee al shigunos*."

Mary took a deep breath and held it, uncertain and nervous. The next few words were a little louder and then the first musical phrase. It was the same modulation the ancient cantors sang thousands of years ago; the same ones young aspiring cantors took years to learn. They flowed from the young man's throat and into the hearts and minds of the congregation.

People sat frozen in time. Nathan's powerful voice, rising, falling, and resonating off the paneled walls, overwhelmed them. He took them to a place they had never been, a place where the ancients went to sing.

Mary, her mouth opening and closing as if in a trance, had not the slightest notion her son possessed not only the voice but also the presence to suddenly be the focus of attention.

More than an hour had passed; the unexpected look of joy on everyone's face made it clear no one wanted Nathan to stop, no one except Manny.

Nathan closed his eyes; the words he had memorized, it was their meaning that only he and Cantor Green understood.

The good cantor had heard Nathan sing his *maftir* a hundred times before, but this time he wasn't singing to him, he was singing to God. In all this time he had never felt this way about any student. His own calling was one of resignation; his parents insisted he follow in his father's footsteps. Nathan's calling was completely different. No one could learn what Nathan had learned in such a short time without God's help.

Nathan had talked to God. He had searched for him and found him, and now God was listening.

His final modulation was warm and comforting, and although he was saying goodbye, this was not the end. Each worshiper had traveled to the edge of the universe; now they waited for Nathan to bring them home, as if they were being led out of the darkness and into the light.

He knew God had listened; he could feel him, he was all around him. Here, in prayer, among his people, this is where he belonged.

Bessy made gefilte fish and *chrane*. The reception for the few invited guests and the numerous members of the congregation took place in the basement beneath the temple floor. Nathan stood with Cantor Green and his wife, surrounded by loyal members of Rabbi Green's congregation.

"This is a monumental day," said one.

"I can't explain how wonderful I feel," said another.

"Mister Roth, Mister Roth!" The cantor was waiving at Manny, beckoning him to join the group.

"You must be so proud; your son is so wonderful," said the cantor's wife.

"All the papers are in my office waiting for your signature. If you'll follow me," said the cantor.

Cantor Green led Nathan and his father into his office at the back of the synagogue. He held the door open for them to enter, closed it, and once behind his desk opened the white file folder.

"This is your consent form, and here are the financial requirements." The cantor placed the folder in Manny's dampened hands.

"What's this? I never agreed to any of this!" he said, the usual redness beginning to form on Manny's face.

"But, Mister Roth, surely you must know that Nathan's place is with God. There is no doubt that he has been called. He must have the opportunity to complete his training as a rabbi."

"Are you nuts?" Manny was as red as a beet. "You think I want a rabbi in my house, telling me what to do? A kid who can't tie his shoes without crying his head off? You think I'd let a sissy like that make a fool of me? You're out of your mind."

"But, Father, I must go! I want to go! You have to let me go."

"I don't have to let you do anything! You've never done anything except cry. A rabbi...you've got to be kidding. Go! Get outside and tell your mother we're leaving right now."

Nathan sat bent over in the back of Manny's new Oldsmobile with his head hanging down between his knees. Aaron sat next to him and said nothing; in fact, no one spoke all the way back to Vancouver.

Still crimson, the angry lines deepened on Manny's face. *Imagine,* a *little half-breed bastard telling me how to be Jewish; have you ever heard of anything so ridiculous?*

It had been two years since the bar mitzvah; of all the things his father had said and done to him, denying Nathan God was the worst. His hatred for Manny and his brother had sustained him ever since. From that fateful day forward Nathan's life had become focused on getting into as much trouble as he could. There were fist fights at school on a regular basis. Irate fathers showed up at his front door demanding Manny pay for the damage to their child's bicycle, broken nose or swollen cheek. Manny screamed at him constantly, and the louder he screamed the more desperate Nathan became.

It was around three a.m.; Paul Mendlbaum pulled himself up to Nathan's open bedroom window.

"C'mon, Nate, I can't hold on much longer."

"I don't think I want to go tonight, Paul." This was the third time the two boys had stolen their father's cars. Tonight, it was Paul's turn.

"C'mon, Roth, don't chicken out on me now."

Reluctantly, Nathan threw on his hand-me-down cords and T-shirt and crawled out his bedroom window and followed his friend across the back lawn to the alley where Paul had parked the Cadillac.

"Slow down, Paul, the cops will see us."

"OK, OK, relax. I just want to drive by my house for a laugh."

Paul's father was standing in the driveway in his pajamas when he spotted them.

"Oh, God, it's your father!" Nathan shouted.

Paul stepped hard on the accelerator, tailspinning the Cadillac out of control and stopping only when the back wheels caught in the open sewer that ran along the narrow street in front of the house.

Mister Mendlbaum ran up to the car and tried to open the door next to Nathan.

"Get out, Roth!" he shouted.

According to Paul, his father had a worse temper than Manny's.

Paul hit the accelerator, dragging his father to the ground.

"You better go back, Paul. We can't hide and there's nowhere to run."

"Shit!" Out on the main street Paul screamed in horror. His father was right behind him. Paul shook from fear as the Cadillac picked up speed and raced along the deserted street.

"Stop, Paul! Paul! Please, Paul!" Nathan shouted.

Down the steep hill the Cadillac raced, faster and faster.

"Paul! You have to stop! You're going to kill us!"

Paul's fear had overtaken him. His eyes glazed; he had no sense of reality.

"Paul!" Nathan covered his face with both arms; it was too late. The red pickup never knew what hit it. The Cadillac sped through the intersection and crashed into the passenger side of the small truck, raising it twenty feet off the ground and sending it flying through the darkness. The Cadillac spun around several times, breaking the axle and flipping over onto the roof as it continued through the intersection, and finally slamming into a telephone pole on the far side.

Jack Medlebaum ran to the smoldering Cadillac. His son's body lay beneath the steering wheel. The bottom rung of the telephone pole had caught Paul in the temple; he was dead.

Nathan lay upside down with his head touching the roof; he was unconscious but completely and miraculously unhurt.

Chapter Nine

Two years in university and failing everything but political science and military history, Aaron accepted Manny's offer to come to work in the factory.

Aaron had always been a straight-A student in high school. President of his graduating class and the student council, voted "most likely to succeed," it was obvious everyone thought Aaron was destined for greatness. Manny hoped it would be medicine or maybe law, but when at university he found out that Aaron spent more time playing bridge than he did studying, another year's tuition wouldn't be wasted.

Aaron could recite whole passages and pages of text in any of his subjects at college, but somehow he wasn't able to put them into practice. At first Manny was impressed with Aaron's ability to quote the appropriate method to use for business, making him vice president of the company, but it became apparent he was unable to understand or implement any of them.

Depressed and angry, Aaron eventually refused to spend any more time in the factory than was absolutely necessary, opting instead to devote his time to fast cars and horse jumping. His friends came from fine gentile families, all with enough money to make Aaron envious of their position and wealth.

A few months into the job, Manny sat behind Aaron's desk furious that Aaron was not at work. As he began to open the numerous envelopes addressed to Aaron care of Roth Enterprises, he realized the extent of his son's irresponsibility. Each statement requested or demanded that Aaron's overdue account for feed or automotive parts for the Alpha be paid, or else. Manny hit the roof; the bills added up to twenty thousand dollars, and added to Aaron's decision to order ten year's worth of factory order forms, it was the last straw.

"There isn't enough room to store them let alone use them. Are you completely nuts?" Manny screamed. "Who told you to do this? Who told you could run up bills for this kind of money? Are you a complete idiot?"

Aaron didn't answer; he simply walked out of his father's office and wasn't heard from again until he called home six months later.

It was six in the morning when the phone rang.

"Hello, Mom, it's me."

"Aaron! Where have you been? I've been worried sick."

"I'm sorry, Mom. I just had to leave."

"Well, at least you're alive Where are you?"

"I'm in Centralia, Ontario. I'll be home tomorrow; can someone pick me up?"

"Where, Aaron? Where will someone pick you up?"

"At the air force base; it's in Richmond."

"The air force base? What are you doing at an air force base?"

"I'm a jet pilot, Mom. An air force pilot. You can call me Flying Officer Aaron Roth now."

"I can't leave the house, Aaron," she said. "I'll have to ask Nathan if he'd pick you up."

"Nathan! Wow, I guess he's driving now."

"Only when your father isn't in town," she replied.

Nathan stood waiting and watched as his brother rounded the corner of the barracks. He was wearing a Royal Canadian Air Force flight uniform and holding a helmet under his arm. Suddenly there was a loud shout. "Attention!" About twenty enlisted men resting on the grassy area next to the one-story building jumped to attention and saluted as Aaron walked by. Aaron returned their salutes, but he was clearly focused on his little brother.

Nathan never thought he would see the day when he had anything but contempt for his tormentor, but there he was, right in front of him, smiling and shaking his hand.

"Well, little brother, what do you think?"

Nathan couldn't begin to imagine what he thought as he looked into the cockpit of Canada's fastest jet aircraft.

"Here; put your left foot there and then the right; that's it."

"Wow! This is amazing. You can really fly this thing?"

Flying Officer N. Roth had excelled. As dim witted as Aaron appeared as a business man, he was as close to a genius as anyone when it came to understanding and implementing the fundamentals of flying at supersonic speed. He had set academic records in each and every segment of his training. By the time he had finished his first tour, he had written two books, several strategic outlines and recommendations on night flying procedures—all at the behest of his commanding officer. His height was the only thing that almost stopped him from becoming a jet pilot in the first place. At five foot six and three quarters, Aaron was a quarter inch under the regulation height, but with some strategic planning and some sneaky ingenuity, he rigged the seat in the trainer so as to give the illusion he was taller than he actually was, and no one was ever the wiser.

"Slow down, will ya, Nathan? These things are too close to the ground." Nathan lifted his foot and slowed the Impala convertible, Manny's latest toy.

"What kind of jet pilot are you, anyway?" Nathan laughed. "You afraid of a little speed?"

"I guess I am, little brother. Up there, there's no one to run into."

Aaron had changed. Nathan didn't know what it was that miraculously transformed him, but whatever it was instantly instilled a feeling of pride he had never known before. It felt new and it felt good. *This is what it feels like to have a brother.*

"I can only stay a few days," he said. Aaron didn't actually expect to run into his father but now that he had, he tried desperately to think of ways to shorten his visit.

"I've got to straighten out a few things I should have done before I left; you understand, Father?"

It was only coincidence that Manny suddenly returned home just hours after Aaron. Like Nathan, Manny was filled with pride, only he just wouldn't tell anyone, especially Aaron. *If Aaron had only worked this hard in the factory.* But then suddenly it hit him; his father was a soldier. Of course his namesake should be a soldier too. Unfortunately, Aaron left before Manny had a chance to tell his eldest son how proud he truly was, although it wouldn't have mattered. The last thing Aaron wanted was to spend a moment longer with his father than he had to, and a moment was all he would ever give him.

Sadly, Nathan handed his brother the bag from the trunk of the car.

"I'm so proud of you, Aaron," Nathan said. "I've told everyone I know. When can I visit you? I've got to get away, Aaron. I can't stand living in the house with him. He never stops. He gets louder and drunker every day. I don't talk to him, and he couldn't care less if I did."

"I wish I could tell you, Nathan, I really do, but the military doesn't give you a choice. I'll let you know when I can, I promise."

Aaron wanted to comfort his little brother but there was no time. He couldn't say where he was going, just something about the Canada's Official Secrets Act.

Nathan watched as his brother's jet climbed to thirty thousand feet and disappeared behind the clouds. He wouldn't see his brother again for five more years.

It was 1962.

Chapter Ten

Mary had been in the bathroom for more an hour as Nathan stood in the hallway and called to her.

"Mom, are you all right?"

She was standing in front of the mirror trying to stop the blood from oozing out the hole in her forehead. It just wouldn't heal; she changed the Elastoplast dressing almost every day, something the doctors told her not to do. The deep wound was a constant irritation; it was a wound of sorrows, and Mary had convinced herself that it was there to remind her of what a mess she had made of her life.

"Mom…please, Mom."

"I'm fine, Nathan. Go away! I'm busy."

She could look at herself now, at least for as long as it took to change the bandages. She dyed her hair blonde, and with the right amount of makeup she didn't look nearly as bad. In fact, she was getting pretty good at disguising the scars; even Leo made a point of telling her how nice she looked, which was going to make it harder for her to tell him she wanted to quit. She had received a phone call from a friend who suggested she get involved in a musical theatre group playing the piano as backup to staged presentations for children. She did, and before long Mary's extraordinary talent came to the attention of the theatre's musical director.

"Mary, could you write a short jingle?" she asked. "One with words that Red Riding Hood could sing on her way to her grandmother's house? Nothing too difficult; just something the children could sing along to."

"I don't know, Jill. I've never written anything before."

"Oh, c'mon, Mary, give it a try. You won't know if you don't try, right?"

That night Mary sat at the upright piano and stared at the keys. She didn't respond to Nathan or Manny the entire evening, but around midnight she played the short, sweet and catchy melody she had written in her head. She played it only once, walked to the dinning room table, sat down and wrote the notes on a napkin.

The small theatre only seated fifty. The smallest children sat with their legs crossed on the floor in front of the actors. Adults with older children sat behind them in the two raised sections. Mary sat at the piano at stage right; the upright piano was slightly angled, preventing her from being seen by the audience. It was the opening for the second act. Little Red was knocking on her grandmother's front door.

One, two, three, Grandmamma, it's me. Little Red Riding Hood has come to tea. When I count four, open up the door, one...two...three...four.

It took everyone by surprise, even Mary. Suddenly every one in the little theatre was singing the charming melody. Everyone felt the magic in the little song, so simple yet so haunting. People left the theatre humming and singing it over and over again. Outside the theatre some four-year-old children were shouting out the words to see who could sing them the loudest.

Mary was still at the piano as Jill Clayburn stood staring at her from the opposite end of the stage near the back. She was thinking about what had happened. *Such a simple song, nothing really. Anyone could have come up with that. My God, I don't see what everybody went crazy about. You'd think she was Beethoven or something.*

The envious director tapped Mary on the shoulder, startling her.

"Well, Mary, that went over well," she said. "Do you think you could write a few more little songs?"

From a few little songs came her first manuscript, an original play with music and lyrics being sung to an adaptation of a well-know fairytale. Colorful new characters that no one ever heard of before were thrown in, giving the old tale new life. The music came alive on stage and, like before, stayed with the audiences for hours afterwards.

The marquee outside the theatre read: Jill Clayburn presents *The Three Bears*. At the bottom in small letters it said, "Mary Roth on piano."

Of course everyone thought Jill Clayburn had written the play as well as the music, something that Jill couldn't bring herself to deny. After all, if it wasn't for her, Mary wouldn't even have a job in the first place.

After three more years and five new plays, all of them written by Mary, no one knew. Mary was so busy writing she didn't concern herself with the rewards; her passion for excellence made her blind to the obvious—Jill Clayburn was becoming famous and Mary didn't even notice.

It was after the last performance of the season. Jill tried to avoid her, but Mary caught her off-guard.

"Oh, Mary, I didn't see you. Sorry, I can't talk now; have to get to the airport."

"Where are you going?" Mary asked. "I thought we were going to talk about the *Pied Piper*?

"I'm sorry, Mary. I'm off to the Toronto opening of *Hansel and Gretel*," she said. "I'll be gone for a week; we can talk about the *Pied Piper* when I get back."

"*Hansel and Gretel*! Did someone write another *Hansel and Gretel*?" Mary asked.

"Why, of course not. It's our *Hansel and Gretel*."

"Our *Hansel and Gretel*? You mean my *Hansel and Gretel*, don't you?"

"Uh, yes, if you like, Mary, your *Hansel and Gretel*." The cat was out of the bag.

"You sold my play to another company without my permission?"

"Well, it wouldn't be anything without me. Anyway, I don't think I need your permission."

"You most certainly do! I can't believe you would do such a thing, Jill, but since you have, you will be hearing from my lawyer. Shame on you, Jill!"

Mary had caught on to Jill's betrayal just in time. It wasn't soon enough to stop the play from being performed in front of two thousand people at Toronto's O'Keefe Centre, but in time to have the marquee changed and the royalty sent to her, and not to Jill Clayburn.

The O'Keefe Centre Theatre in downtown Toronto was all but deserted, just a few stagehands walking hurriedly back and forth across the massive stage.

Val Belkin remained seated in his usual centre aisle seat. The tingles still lingered as a young blonde woman touched his shoulder.

"Mister Belkin…we'll be closing up now. Do you want me to call you a cab or something?"

"Uh, yes, I mean, no. I think I'll walk a little, thanks."

Val had been in a semi-conscious state ever since the opening curtain. *The story was wonderful; how can you go wrong with gingerbread and old witches.* But it was the music that took him along the wooded path and down the hill to the enchanted forest. It was the music that rose from the pit and fell over him giving him the tingles. He always got the tingles; that's how he knew. He'd produced dozens of musicals but this one was different. He had been less than enthusiastic when he first heard it was an original adaptation of a fairytale. *I should have known that Clayburn woman was a phony. True artists and composers are never that pushy.*

Val left the theatre and walked several blocks before realizing where he was. He whistled and hummed Mary's haunting melodies over and over again. *I can't remember the last time I whistled.* By the time he reached Bloor Street and caught a cab he had made up his mind. *I've got to meet Mary Roth.* The following day Val placed the call to Vancouver.

"Mary, this is Val Belkin. Can you hear me?" There was an annoying hissing sound that hung in the background.

"Yes, I can hear you. I'm sorry, who is this?"

"Val Belkin, Mary, I produced your play."

"Oh, of course, Val Belkin...yes, how foolish of me."

"Not at all, Mary. Not at all. Mary?"

"Yes, Val."

"I want to produce your next play. Are you working on anything right now?"

"Well, yes, Val, I am; just about finished in fact."

He couldn't hide his excitement.

"Mary, you must let me have it; you must! I insist."

Mary was flattered; no one of importance had shown much interest in her before.

"I can send you the music; I'm still working on the script."

"What's it called, Mary? I mean, what's it about? Is it a fairytale, like *Hansel*?"

"Yes, it's called *Hamlin*. It's about the Pied Piper of Hamlin."

"Hamlin, Pied Piper...of course, the Pied Piper. Oh, Mary, this is too good," he said, his breathing becoming more rapid and difficult. Mary could tell he was struggling for air. Val had suffered his whole life with asthma and it wasn't getting any better.

"Mary, have you made copies? Or better still, can you record the music and send it to me as soon as you can?"

"I imagine I could, yes...I know someone who could record me on the piano; would that be OK?"

"That would be perfect, Mary. I can't wait."

Val pushed down the two keys of the recorder and waited for Mary's low raspy voice to make the introduction;

"*Hamlin*: a musical adaptation by Mary Roth. Overture to Act One." Val could feel his heart pounding as Mary began to play. It was everything he hoped, only better. The music, like always, gave him the goose bumps first, then the tingles. He listened to one melody after another, each more haunting and more enchanting than the last. Mary occasionally stopped playing to add a smattering of dialogue before moving on through the second act and ending with the finale.

The loud click of the recorder at the end of the tape jolted him back to reality. He had visualized each scene as it unfolded on stage. There was tragedy one minute and joy and happiness the next; it was only a fairytale meant for children, but such music could turn the heart of any adult.

Mary answered the phone on the first ring. Val didn't even wait for her to say hello.

"Mary, it's simply genius! It's better than anything Disney has done. In fact, with your permission, I want to approach them."

"Disney! Are you sure, Val?" The telephone connection was the worst yet.

Mary and Val talked every day for two weeks. Even though they had never met, they talked to each other as if they had been friends for years. Mary's tormented life with an abusive husband didn't seem nearly as tragic when Val told her of his own unhappy marriage.

"Maybe it's time you thought about life without Manny," he said. "Maybe it would be easier for Nathan as well."

Val called back a few days later with the good news.

"Disney wants it, Mary. They've asked me to bring you to Hollywood, and they want everything: you, the script, and of course the music. I think they're thinking a full-length animated film, and I get to produce it. Isn't this wonderful, Mary?" Mary didn't answer. "Mary, did you hear me? We're going to California."

"Yes, Val, I heard you. I don't think I'm cut out for California, Val."

"Don't be ridiculous, Mary. I'll be in Vancouver the day after tomorrow; we'll plan our strategy. Those Disney guys might think we're a couple of dummies, so we need to be prepared. I'll call you as soon as I check-in. Goodbye, Mary."

It was almost eight o'clock; the canopied hotel entrance was only partially effective—avoiding the pelting rain was a way of life in this town. Val held the collar of his raincoat over his ears and made a dash for the cab.

"Driver, step on it, will ya please?"

An hour and two martinis later, Val was frantic; it was past nine and there was no sign of Mary. He began thinking about Mary's sudden change of attitude since he told her about Disney. An abusive husband and repressed genius, the potential for tragedy was obvious; he had to find her. They had never met but he already loved her.

Mary's trembling made it impossible; she'd been in front of the mirror for two hours as pieces of blood-soaked gauze lay at her feet. A small bottle of liquid makeup had fallen into the sink, spilling out and leaving Mary without the possibility of leaving the house, never mind meeting Val.

She had failed once again to stop the bleeding; each time she thought she had, by the time she put her makeup back on, the bleeding would start its journey once again down the crease in her forehead and along the side of her nose.

"Mom…Mom! Do you know what time it is?" Nathan had just come home and knew about his mother's plans to meet Mister Belkin for dinner.

"Go away, Nathan, please!"

"But, Mom, what about Mister Belkin? You were supposed to meet him…Mom?"

The door chimes rang out as Nathan continued to plead with her. "Mom, there's someone at the door. I'll be right back, OK?

"OK, Nathan."

Val was soaked clean through.

"Hello, Nathan. I'm Val Belkin. Is your mother home? I've been worried about her, and well, no one answered the phone. I just had to come. Is she here? Can I come in?"

"I think you'd better, Mister Belkin; she's not doing too well."

Nathan thought he'd be much older; he had dark curly hair and dark eyes. The fact that he was kind of courting his mother was, at that moment, peculiar, to say the least.

"Please, Mister Belkin, you're drenched." Nathan took Val's coat and hat and led him into the kitchen.

"Where's Mary, Nathan? Why didn't she meet me?"

"She couldn't meet you, Mister Belkin. She was afraid you wouldn't understand."

"Understand what? We've been talking about this for weeks; everything's arranged. Mary is going to be famous."

"You see, that's it, Mister Belkin; she can't be famous. People will want to see her, and well, she doesn't want to be seen."

"What do you mean she doesn't want to be seen? Why not for goodness sake?"

"Mister Belkin, my mom doesn't want anyone to see her face. She just couldn't take it."

"What the heck are you talking about? She never said anything to me about not wanting to be seen."

"She didn't want to disappoint you, Mister Belkin. She didn't know how to tell you, and well, I guess she was hoping for a miracle, like the ones in her stories."

"Nathan, for God's sake, will you tell me what you're talking about?"

"Her face, Mister Belkin; my mom's face is scared all over. She wears bandages to stop the bleeding. She just didn't want you to see her. She's so afraid, and well, perhaps it would be better if you let her be."

Val jumped off his chair and walked out of the kitchen and down the hall towards the bathroom.

"Mary, Mary Roth? Where are you? Are you in there? You get out here right this moment! Do you hear me?"

Val pounded repeatedly on the locked door.

"Oh, Val, go away! I can't see you….please go away."

"Mary Roth! I didn't come all this way to have you tell me you can't look at me. Nathan has told me about your face. I can't believe you'd think that would make a pinch of difference to me. Now you come out of there right this minute, or I'll break down this door!"

Mary opened the door; the bleeding had stopped but her makeup was all over the place. They looked at each other for only an instant; Val took her and held her in his arms, stroking the back of her head, telling her everything was going to be all right.

"It's all right now, Mary," he said. "You never have to be afraid ever again."

Nathan's own tears left little doubt; his own father would never make his mother this happy.

Chapter Eleven

Little Bessy Sugerman opened her apartment door and welcomed her grandson.

"Such a good boy," she said, pinching his cheek.

She took the package of pastries Nathan had brought and placed a few of them on a plate in front of him.

"Now, tell Bubba, how's your father?"

"I really don't know how he is, Bubba. He doesn't talk to me."

"What do you mean he doesn't talk to you? What father doesn't talk to such a good boy?"

Nathan felt sorry for his grandmother. Now three times a widow, Bessy had moved to Vancouver to be closer to her son, only her son never went to see her. Nathan brought her pastry once or twice a week and listened while Bessy told him stories about his grandfather and her beloved captain who saved her and Rachel from the Russian assassins.

Nathan wiped the tears from her cheek as the memories of her parents brought back the pain and suffering of all the Jews who were persecuted by their Christian masters. She was so little, thought Nathan. How could someone so small have lived through the horror of it all? He sat for hours with her just listening. Even when Bessy spoke in Yiddish and tried to fool him, Nathan wasn't fooled; somehow he understood every word she said.

"Such a *mench,*" she said. "How do you know what I said?" she asked.

"You taught me, Bubba. I understand everything you say."

"Then understand this, Nathan. Your father lost his own father at thirteen; he really doesn't know about children. He had to be a man and go to work to support the family. It was very hard for him."

"I know it was hard, Bubba, but not as hard as it is for me and my mom. He is cruel, Bubba, very cruel. I don't want to talk about him, Bubba, please. Tell me more about my grandfather and the blacksmith shop. Tell me again how much you loved him."

The small, darkened movie house at the south end of the city was full to capacity. Nathan really didn't want to go, but after Leo told him his old friends from camp would be there, he couldn't refuse.

He sat staring at the screen. Hundreds, no, thousands of pounds of lifeless flesh was piled high, being bulldozed into gaping holes in the earth. He saw them with their eyes still open, looking into the camera and crying out to a silent world. He felt the phlegm gathering at the back of his throat as he watched the film and photographs of the Nazi genocide. He crouched deeper into the velvet chair as the horror of it unfolded in front of him. It was more than he could stand. Covering his mouth and bent over from the pain in his stomach, Nathan ran up the aisle and out of the theatre.

Squatting by the curb, he spewed the final remnants of his dinner. Nothing was left except the pain. *Oh, God, how could you let this happen to my people? What have we done to make you hate us so?* He tried to throw up again but nothing came out. *Why did Leo want me to see those damn pictures?*

Nathan barely finished high school; by grade nine, everyone believed Nathan lacked the intelligence and academic ability to go to college. "You should learn a trade," Manny said. "I'll get you a job in a Toronto factory; just don't embarrass me." It was one of the few times Manny showed even the slightest interest in what Nathan might do with his life.

A month short of his eighteenth birthday, Nathan left Vancouver and traveled across Canada by train—it was a vast and beautiful country. Sitting in the observation car, Nathan felt as if the world he had known was about to change. The days of crying as his father berated him were over, and although the job Manny had arranged for him was nothing more than sweeping floors and stacking bolts of cloth, the expectation of real happiness for the first time filled him with joy.

"Hey, Roth, you check off those linings against the invoice?" The tone of his voice and the look of disgust were all too familiar to Nathan.

Jack Greenspan was an acquaintance of Manny's from the old days; the arrogant and overweight manufacturer had made no effort to help Nathan find a place to live as Manny had asked. Jack had picked him up at the train station and brought him to his home in north Toronto. "Don't get too comfortable, kid," he said. "You can only stay a week."

Jack's wife Edna was shy and hardly spoke to anyone, especially her husband. Alone most of the time, she spent her days caring for and loving her twin nine-year-old boys. Lewis and Marty were slightly retarded, a handicap their father blamed on her and her immigrant parents. Edna and the boys quickly grew fond of their new houseguest. He took the twins for long walks to the park and taught them to throw and catch a baseball. He read to them and tucked them in at night, and in the mornings they jumped on his bed and wrestled with him until their fathered hollered at them to stop. It was love at first sight. By week's end, Edna also had come out of her shell and was now joining in the fun.

Jack Greenspan threw the evening paper on the living room coffee table, destroying the puzzle the boys and Nathan were working on.

"You will have to leave tomorrow," he said. "You start work on Monday."

Later that night, Nathan could hear Jack and Edna quarreling upstairs.

"Just keep your mouth shut, woman!" he shouted. "He is ruining the boys! They think they're fine."

"They are fine," she said, "and they love him. They have never been happier and neither have I."

"Swell, maybe you should be looking for a place to live too."

The next morning no one came to wake him. Upstairs on the kitchen counter Nathan found a note addressed to him.

> *Nathan,*
> *We have gone away for the weekend. Attached is a news clipping with all the rooms available in the city. I suggest you be in one of them by the time we get back.*

That Monday Nathan waited at the entrance as Jack Greenspan opened the door to the factory. It was day one; the factory was closed for the holidays and only Jack and a few others, including Nathan, were working.

It was late in the afternoon when Jack took the paper invoice from Nathan, examined it and began his attack.

"I don't think you did check the invoice, did you, Roth?"

Nathan didn't like being called a liar, and since he had already checked the invoice twice, he glared back at his employer.

"I've checked it twice; the shipment is short two pieces and that is the truth."

"You're a damn liar! Aren't you, Roth? Nothing but a damn liar!"

Nathan stood in front of Jack Greenspan and looked into the hateful eyes of the intolerant man.

"You are the worst excuse for a husband and father I've ever seen," he said. "You don't deserve a wife; you certainly don't deserve your wonderful children."

"Look, you little prick!" Greenspan shouted. "Get out! Or I'll kick the shit out of you." Nathan didn't take his eyes off him "Get out!" he screamed again, and reached for Nathan's throat. Before he knew what hit him, Jack Greenspan lay face down on the cement floor—so much for Mister Greenspan and Nathan's first job.

Nathan found the seven-dollar-a-week room on the top floor of an old rooming house in Toronto's Little Europe. The West Islington neighborhood was home to thousands of new immigrants; each narrow side street was like a small country in itself. Eastern Europeans were on one street; Italians, Greeks and Turks on another. The Poles and Hungarians along with the Latvians and Lithuanians made up the rest. People from all over the world were eking out a living in all manner of ways.

Islington Avenue went for miles. A thousand storefronts on both sides, with the sound of streetcars and their iron wheels grinding against their metal rails made normal conversation impossible. If you wanted to talk you had an espresso or a regular coffee in one of a thousand restaurants, each one different, and in each one men sat telling tales of the atrocities and horrors they endured at the hands of the Nazi dictator.

Nathan had been living in the third floor room for a week when he finally met the landlord's wife.

"You speak Lithuanian!" she said. "How is it you can speak this?"

"My grandmother taught me," Nathan said.

"Your grandmother taught you? My husband didn't tell me you were Lithuanian. My God! This changes everything."

Mister Sharnofsky hadn't asked him where he was from or who his parents were. Now that everyone knew, he was suddenly welcomed with open and loving arms.

Otto Sharnofsky was tall and thin with short red hair. Marcia Sharnofsky was twice the size of her husband; she had an enormous smile and even larger bosoms, accentuated further by her tight buttoned-up dress. Both were already middle aged when they immigrated to Canada in 1948. They worked hard and built a new life after the one they had was ripped away by the Nazis.

That night, Nathan and the rest of the family sat around the kitchen table as Nathan explained his recent altercation with Mister Greenspan. Missus Sharnofsky placed the bowl of soup in front of him and patted his shoulder.

"You will come and work in the restaurant tomorrow. We will figure out what else you will do later. Now eat; you're too thin."

The sign over the door read *Sharnofsky's*. Nathan waited tables and learned how to use the espresso machine; no easy task, since Otto wouldn't hear of replacing the old relic. "My father made coffee with it and I will make coffee with it," he said.

By month's end Nathan had met and made friends with dozens of people in the neighborhood, if for no other reason than his uncanny ability to understand and speak their language.

The double-front restaurant was busier than ever. It wasn't long before everyone heard of the handsome young stranger from Vancouver. It was puzzling; even Nathan didn't understand how he had learned so many languages. It had become a popular topic and one that began as interesting conversation, but in the days ahead it turned into much more. Everyone started to believe Nathan was blessed and had come for a reason, a reason only God could know.

More and more people came just so they could order something in their own language. Owners of other restaurants came to eat and talk to Nathan, wishing like hell they had found him first.

It took at least an hour for Nathan to walk the two blocks between the restaurant and the rooming house. He couldn't resist; he loved to talk to them, all of them.

"*Buon giorno*, Nathan!"
"*Come siete*, Don D'Angelo?"
"*Bene*, Nathan!"

Tony D'Angelo was a big and burly Italian who owned three restaurants in the neighborhood. The self-appointed patriarch of the Italian community and suspected mafia boss also enjoyed Nathan's company.

"C'mon, Nathan, you sure your parents didn't come from Sicily?"

"I'm sure, Don D'Angelo. No Roths in Italy, as far as I know."

"Nathan, my charming boy, I want you to come and work a for me. I'll pay you double," he said, putting his arm around Nathan's shoulder.

"I am deeply grateful, Don D'Angelo, but would you want me to break the hearts of my family? There are too many broken hearts already, aren't there, Don D'Angelo?"

"Sì, Nathan, far too many. You like pasta, Nathan? Come; have some pasta with old Tony, OK?"

"OK, Don D'Angelo, but only one bowl today, OK?"

"OK, *paisan*, just a one bowl."

Weeks turned into months. The Sharnofskys and hundreds of others grew to love him, and Nathan loved them too. They were his family now, all of them. This is where he was meant to be.

Chapter Twelve

Manny propped himself up against the sofa pillows; at least he could watch the Friday night fights without her banging on the piano. Gone, just like that, no explanation, nothing. He didn't even know where she was. Thank God the house was in his name; good thing since he had to sell it anyway. The bank had denied his last loan request and his partner ran out on him after managing to embezzle half a million dollars before he disappeared. Forty thousand in unpaid taxes and not enough orders to keep the factory open, Manny closed the doors forever. With nothing left, his only option was to talk to his mother.

The elevator was still out of service as Bessy struggled up the stairs to her third floor apartment. Exhausted, she fell gently into her easy chair and laid her head back. *A nap would be perfect.* As she was about to doze off there was a knock on the door.

"It's me, Mom, Manny."

"Manny?"

Out of breathe and as red as a tomato, Manny opened the door with his own key.

"What? You just let yourself in? You can't wait a second?" Bessy sat back down and sighed.

"I have to sell the farm, Mother," he said in Yiddish—he thought it would be easier.

"Sell the farm? Are you crazy? I will not sell the farm…ever! It is leased to wonderful people. I would never sell the farm."

"Mother, you don't understand. I've lost the factory and my house. I need money to get back on the road, so we have to sell the farm and that's that."

Bessy tried to stand; her hand slipped as she tried to grip the arm of the easy chair before falling back. A sharp pain went up her arm and into her chest and her willingness to argue with Manny had left her. The pain intensified as she thought of her grandson. *Nathan…such a good boy.*

Bessy Roth Sugerman died on April 17, 1964; she was eighty-one years old.

Nathan sat alone at the far end of the pew and as far away as he could get from his father. The plain grey casket lay on the raised platform in front of him. Many people came, some from as far away as Florida and South America. Nathan assumed they were relatives. He wasn't really interested in meeting them and as far as he could tell they weren't interested in meeting him either. *Just as well, they would just ask stupid questions and talk to me as if I were a child.*

Nathan hadn't stopped crying for days. Even Lizzy seemed genuinely concerned, something totally unlike her. She had called Nathan in Toronto with the news and offered to buy his plane ticket. He was thankful but told her he had saved enough to buy his own.

"Nathan," Rabbi Green whispered in his ear, "it's time." Nathan and five others lifted the casket and proceeded to carry it outside and into the waiting hearse. It was an hour's drive to the cemetery and although he looked for an alternative, he had no choice but to ride in the limo with the family.

Manny sat directly across from him, his face red and swollen. Aunt Dina, as always, led the conversation, trying her best to ease everyone's sorrow.

"How do you like Toronto, Nathan?" she asked.

Nathan tried to answer, but only glanced at her briefly without speaking.

A light rain fell around the gathering as they stood over the open grave. Cantor Green held the prayer book as Manny began to read the prayer for the dead. He was shaking and crying and had to be supported on both sides by Lizzy and Aunt Dina. Nathan knew his father didn't know the meaning of the words he was reading and wished he would stop. Suddenly Manny began to choke, unable to control his grief and unable to recite the prayer. Cantor Green looked at Nathan and motioned to him to begin where his father left off.

With tear-soaked eyes Nathan ended his prayer and opened the piece of paper he took from his jacket and began to read.

"There are no ghosts upon the earth; our eyes are closed to them. They are shadows of the heart, closer now than before. Sweet fragrances she gives to me to help me understand it is love I smell. It covers me so I can see what

I cannot touch. She holds me tight, so I can sleep. Her gentle breath upon my face, I need not look to see. I feel her now; it's clear to me; she will never leave my mind, of this I'm sure. What's that I hear, a father's voice, a sister, mother too, a gathering of kind, a home for you. I love you, Bubba. I can say it freely. I love you, Bubba. I know you hear me.

Chapter Thirteen

"It seems we overbooked this flight; hmm, how does first-class sound?" The attractive ticket agent handed Nathan his boarding pass.

"Have a nice flight, Mister Roth," she said.

"Huh?" No one had ever called him Mister Roth before. He looked behind to see if his father had followed him to the airport. "Uh, oh yes, thanks."

On board, Nathan placed his small bag in the overhead compartment and took his seat next to the window.

"Would you like some champagne before takeoff, sir?" the young stewardess said, as she held the opened bottle so he could see the label.

"Sure, why not?"

She obviously thought a man in a suit was automatically twenty-one. He took the champagne glass from her and held it as she poured.

"Will there be anything else, sir?" she asked.

"I'll have one of those, miss, if you don't mind," said the giant standing behind the stewardess. He had brown skin and wore a black suit with a white clerical collar.

"Father Nathanial Brighton, young man, and you are?" The giant priest held out his enormous hand; Nathan took it and marveled at how small his own hand was in comparison.

"Nathan Roth, Father."

"Well, well, isn't that a coincidence."

Father Nathanial took his seat and fell into it, rocking the entire front section of the plane.

"Where doth thou goest, young Nathan?"

"Back to Toronto, Father," he said. Nathan's eyes were closed as he answered.

"I sense sadness in thee. Are thee in mourning?" he asked.

"My grandmother, Father."

Nathan opened his eyes and wiped away a tear with the back of his hand.

"You loved her, my son?"

"I love her still, Father."

A minute passed as the priest studied his companion.

"What faith are thee, my son?"

"I'm Jewish, Father."

"Ah, yes, brothers and sisters of Abraham and Isaac; ancient souls resting in Christ."

The priest unbuttoned his jacket displaying a large silver cross that hung around his neck. He held it, closed his eyes and prayed. *"Heavenly Father, we beseech Thee, lessen young Nathan's pain. Show him Your love and bring peace where there is sadness. Give him strength and lighten his sorrow. In the name of the Father, the Son, and the Holy Spirit, amen."*

"Tell me about Christ, Father. May I call you, Father?" he said. "Tell me about Jesus."

For the next two hours Father Brighton quoted excerpts and sayings from the New Testament. Nathan listened intensely as Father Brighton gave him a crash course in Catholicism. By the time they were over Winnipeg, Nathan had more questions than answers. He realized it would be improper and impolite to argue over anything Father Brighton had told him, but sensing the priest was waiting for him to say something, he decided to be as careful as he could so not to offend him.

"It's our faith that binds us together, don't you agree, Father?"

"What exactly do you mean, my son?"

"So many people, so many religions, and all of them saying the same thing. It's what's so common to us all. I wonder if God intended it that way. What do you think, Father?"

The giant priest took another sip before attempting to answer. He wasn't prepared for such a question; how could he possibly know what God intended.

By the time the captain announced their decent, Father Brighton had many more answers than questions.

The priest listened to every word as Nathan told him how he felt about his beloved grandmother.

"She was my connection to God," he said. "I felt closer to Him when I was with her."

Father Brighton touched Nathan's hand.

"You are surely blessed, young Nathan. I know not what God has in store for thee, but I am certain He will tell us soon enough."

Nathan stepped off the streetcar a block too soon; the walk would do him good; besides, a few friendly faces was just what he needed. Oddly, there were none around. Five o'clock and if he didn't know better he would swear Islington had practically shut down. Every other shop window had a closed sign on the door or a note saying "back soon" or "back in five."

The closer he got to Sharnofsky's the quieter it became. Had he missed something? Had something happened during his flight back? He was definitely concerned as he opened the front door of the dimly lit restaurant.

"Surprise! Surprise!"

Nathan jumped a foot off the ground; people, hundreds of them, shouted all at once. He thought the roof was falling and ducked his head as he raised his arms to protect himself.

"Welcome home, Nathan!" Missus Sharnofsky was the first to embrace him. "I missed you so," she said in Lithuanian.

Mister Sharnofsky was next, then the rest of the family, first Milo and then Terra and then Peter. Don D'Angelo pinched and kissed his cheek.

"*Come siete*, paisan I'm very happy you have returned to us."

"It's wonderful to be back with my family, Don D'Angelo."

Mister Sharnofsky turned and looked at the admiring crowd.

"Our Nathan is home! Everybody, eat and drink. It is time for celebration, yes?"

"Yes!" they shouted.

Everyone knew how upset Nathan had been before he left for the funeral. Don D'Angelo spent the entire week telling everyone in advance so no one would miss his homecoming.

"This is a wonderful thing you do for our Nathan, Don D'Angelo," she said. Mrs. Sharnofsky had never cared for the pompous Italian until now.

People came and left, then came back again. No one missed the party. From three blocks in both directions they came, closing their own stores and restaurants early so they wouldn't miss a moment. They ate drank and sang until they could no longer stand—except Nathan, who never cared for alcohol At the end, around two, he said goodbye to Tony, sent the Sharnofskys home, and closed up. He would never forget this wonderful day.

The following morning, Mrs. Sharnofsky called him from the bottom of the stairs.

"Nathan, Nathan!"

"Yes, Mama, what is it?"

"Telephone, it's for you."

"Is it long distance, Mama?" he shouted from the top floor landing.

"No, Nathan, I don't think so."

He held the old corded phone to his ear. "Hello, this is Nathan," he said.

"Boy, you're a tough guy to find. At least you told your mother where you were."

"Leo! It's good to hear your voice."

"You, too, my young friend. Are you free for dinner tonight?"

"Uh, sure, but you'll have to come to the restaurant. I'm working tonight. Actually, I work every night."

Nathan was delighted to introduce Leo to his adopted family and the family seemed delighted to meet him. They sat at the staff table at the back of the restaurant.

"Sorry if this was inconvenient for you, Leo, but as you can see, it's always busy. I just couldn't get away."

"No problem, Nathan. This food is great and, as usual, your loyalty, well, it's admirable."

"So, my mom told you where I was, but you haven't told me why you're here," Nathan inquired.

Leo waited for Mrs. Sharnofsky to clear away the remaining dishes; she was beginning to sense Leo had more on his mind than just an informal visit.

"It might only be a coincidence, Nathan, but the fact that you're here and I'm now the president of the ZOC, well, it's more like destiny than coincidence."

He went on to tell Nathan that the ZOC had bought a piece of property near Sudbury, some three hundred miles north of Toronto, for the purpose of building a summer camp for teenagers. It was similar to Camp Zion but more focused on developing leaders rather than just fun and games.

"When I heard you were here I just had to talk to you about it. The movement needs leaders, Nathan, and there's no one better suited to eventually head up one of a dozen other camps we intend to build. It wouldn't surprise me if you ended up running the national program in a few years. What do you say; will you come? It's only this summer and if you find it's not for you, you'll know in a couple of months. And by the way, we'll cover all your expenses."

"Gee, Leo, I don't know. Can I get back to you?"

"Sure, Nathan, but let me know tomorrow, OK?"

Not entirely pleased with Nathan's promise to "give it some thought," Leo said goodbye to the family and thanked them for a wonderful meal. He opened his wallet and placed some bills on the table. Missus Sharnofsky handed Leo back his money and told him, "Nobody pays if you're a friend of our Nathan."

Mrs. Sharnofsky's intuition was right.

"This man wants to take our Nathan, Papa," she said later.

Mr. Sharnofsky never doubted his wife's intuition. Later that night, Nathan asked for a moment to sit with them.

"It's only for the summer, Mama," he said. "I'll be back the first week in September. I promise."

Mama Sharnofsky did her best not to show how upset she was, but the days leading up to his leaving were very hard on her. He made her breakfast every morning and read to her in the evenings.

No one, including Don D'Angelo, was happy with Nathan's decision.

"I a hope you know what you are doing, my young friend. You just remember, if you a need something, I am a always here."

"Thank you, Don D'Angelo."

"You be careful, *paisan*. Things are not always what they seem, you understand?"

"*Sì*, Don D'Angelo, I'll be careful. I promise."

A week later everything seemed a little less inviting; Leo was not going to be at the camp to meet him, and as he stared out the window of the Greyhound Bus, Nathan's attitude was less than positive.

"This is it, Nathan! Stop two seventeen. You sure this is where they told you to get off?"

"Yep, this is it, George; two seventeen."

The bus driver and Nathan had talked for hours. It was a long trip and Nathan was the last remaining passenger.

"Hope everything works out for you, Nathan."

"You too, George. You tell that son of yours to get back to school, or he'll have to answer to me, OK?"

"OK, Nathan, I'll tell him."

"*Kusenam sapan*, George." Hungarian was always a difficult language, even for Nathan.

He waited by the side of the highway for an hour before the old orange school bus stopped in front of him. The double doors opened and a rough looking man in a white T-shirt asked, "You Nathan Roth?"

"That's me."

"Well, get in. What are you waiting for, Yom Kippur?"

Nathan stepped up and into the bus tossing his knapsack on the seat across from him.

"You might as well relax, chaver," he said. "It's another hour to camp."

Camp Sharavah, according to Leo, was brand-new. As the bus passed through the main gate and up the hill along the dirt road, it was obvious there was nothing new about anything. They passed a number of small buildings that looked like fallout shelters, a baseball diamond overgrown with long grass on the right, and about five acres of hay on the left. He could see a lake on the other side of the hayfield and another smallish building with smoke rising from its chimney. The sun was about to set as the bus stopped at the top of the road in front of a large two-story wooden house. It had dark brown siding, an old slanted cedar shake roof and a wide covered veranda that ran all around the outside.

"Up there," the driver said, as he opened the doors and pointed to the front of the house. Nathan thought the driver was as dumb as they come, considering as he was unable to enter into any form of conversation during the hour and a half bus trip.

As Nathan reached the top of the veranda stairs, he was greeted by the camp's new director.

"Nathan, Nathan Roth. Shalom."

"Shalom alechem," Nathan replied.

"We have been waiting for you all day. What kept you? Never mind, come in, you must be exhausted. Leo has told me so much about you. I feel I know you already."

Nathan guessed David Chechik was around thirty. He had brown eyes, a strong chin, and was built like Hercules. He would find out just how strong he was during hand-to-hand combat training.

"I know you're going to love it here, Nathan," he said. "The dinning hall is over there."

Nathan looked to see the new metal roofed building through the window on the other side of the house.

"The infirmary is over there and the bell tents you'll find as soon as we put them up over in the hay field."

They spoke for fifteen minutes before David suggested Nathan get some sleep.

"You're too late for supper," he said. "If you're really hungry, I can see if there's something Missus Viner can bring you, if you like?"

"That's OK, I'd rather sleep."

"Good idea. There's a lot of work to do tomorrow. Your room is at the top of the stairs on the left. You'll have your own tent as soon as you put it up. Shalom, and good night, Nathan."

By sundown the next day Nathan, David and Sonny, the bus driver, had cleared about an acre of hay and had the first of sixty tents assembled in place. Leo had forgotten to mention that the other hundred and twenty campers weren't arriving until the following week. It was hard work, but the three of them couldn't have been more proud of themselves. Turned out Sonny wasn't all that stupid after all. He had an engineering degree from McGill; without him the camp would be without showers, a shvitz, a proper sewage disposal and a fresh water supply system. David led the team by example, never wavering in his effort to motivate and encourage them to keep at it. "Just one more and we're done, c'mon, guys, we can do it!" he said. By the end of the week Camp Hatikvah did indeed look like a new camp.

They came from across Canada; young men and women recruited by the ZOC and more than anxious to spend an entire summer experiencing and learning what it takes to be a Zionist. Besides being a camp for Jewish teenagers, it was also a camp designed to motivate and encourage them to become leaders in their own communities by rallying local youth in support of the Jewish homeland. Little time was spent on religion and culture; the camp's focus was to create leaders, and in order to do that many children had to forget that they came from wealth and privilege. Now they had to learn self-defense, guerrilla tactics and wilderness survival. With only a compass and canteen in the middle of nowhere, dodging snake infested swamps for two and three days at a time, some kids just couldn't handle it.

"My father would never have let me come if he knew it was going to be like this. I'm out of here."

"This place is worse than the army; I wanna go home."

Some were asked to leave, but in the end a hundred remained committed to the cause; it was the cause that gave those who stayed the incentive to go on.

Cantor Chiem Nishi arrived on day fifteen. Someone at ZOC headquarters got worried that not enough emphasis was being placed on religious doctrine and as much as David Chechik resented the interference, he had no choice but to alter the daily programs to satisfy the cantor.

Nathan and the cantor sat across from each other at an old wooden table on the back veranda of the main house. The cantor had made it his business to find out the religious background of each camper, and Nathan was first on the list.

"Your name is Nathan Roff…correct?" He spoke with a faint lisp.

"Yes, Cantor, Nathan Roth, correct."

"And your father's name is Emanuel, and your mother's maiden name is…"

"Hampton, Mary Hampton." Nathan felt like spelling it for him.

"I see," said the cantor.

Nathan wondered how the old cantor found his mouth, let alone eats with it. His beard was at least a foot long, fifty shades of gray. Nathan suspected a hole with a few rotten teeth lurked somewhere behind the hair. He wore a small black yarmulke that sat perfectly on his bald spot on the top of his head. His eyes were small and black and darted back and forth as he spoke.

"Your mother converted?" Nathan recognized the old man's accent; somewhere near St. Petersburg, he thought.

The old cantor never saw it coming as Nathan suddenly spoke to him in Hebrew.

"My mother is the mother of all that is good in the world," he said.

The old cantor's mouth could now be seen for the first time. It remained open as Nathan continued to speak about his mother and his fondness for his teacher and mentor, Cantor Green.

"You speak Hebrew?" he said "How did you learn? Did your father teach you? Or perhaps, maybe, your grandmother?"

"I'd rather not talk of that, Cantor. In fact, I have no more time today. My self-defense class is about to start; perhaps tomorrow we can talk some more. Good day, Cantor."

Nathan started down the back steps of the veranda stopping halfway, avoiding two small feet that blocked his way. Their eyes met; he couldn't move. She tilted her head wondering what he was looking at.

"You OK? Nathan, isn't it?" she asked.

He still couldn't move, and he couldn't speak either. He tried but nothing came out. Suddenly aware of looking foolish, he stepped to his right and let her pass. He'd seen her before in the dining hall. He even thought she glanced his way once, but he wasn't certain.

Two weeks later the old cantor approached Nathan again.

"Nathan," he said, interrupting one of his classes, "I need to speak to you."

The heavy accent was unmistakable. Nathan turned away from his current task to look at the old cantor.

"Certainly, Cantor. I'll see you on the veranda in an hour. Would that be OK? Or I'll have some time tomorrow."

This was the second or third time Nathan failed to avoid the cantor and his request to speak to him.

"An hour...on the veranda, yes! Good!" he said.

Nathan turned back and resumed coaching the two combatants who were standing in the center of a circle trying to wrestle each other to the ground. David had been a wonderful and efficient instructor. Nathan was a talented student and took to martial arts as if he was born to it.

Cantor Nishi sat at the wooden table looking through some papers as Nathan skipped up the stairs and took a seat.

"Well, isn't it a beautiful day, Rabbi?" he said cheerfully. "Mind you, some of those clouds look a little threatening; what do you think, Rabbi?" It was more appropriate to call the cantor, rabbi; it showed Nathan considered him a teacher, a man to be respected.

The cantor had a lot of time to think about what he wanted to talk to him about, but now that he was in front of him, he didn't know how to start. He just sat there for a couple of minutes not saying anything, just staring into nowhere.

"You wanted to talk to me, Cantor, about something important, maybe?"

"Ah, yes, yes. I have a letter from Cantor Green."

"Cantor Green? Why have you done this?" Nathan demanded.

Cantor Green had responded to Cantor Nishi's request for information about Nathan's religious training and anything else he was willing to share. What he got back was much more than he bargained for. Cantor Green had made his feelings for Nathan very clear; he called him blessed and deeply religious. The cantor also said Nathan possessed an understanding of the faith that contradicted rabbinical teachings, and he advised Cantor Nishi not to challenge Nathan's beliefs, or he might begin to doubt his own.

"I have chosen you to lead sechut," he said. The old cantor blurted it out as if no one was listening.

Nathan was quick to answer.

"I'm sure there are others who are far more qualified than I, Cantor. Besides, I'm sure I'm too busy to..."

"Yes, that's it!" the cantor said, ignoring Nathan's response. "The topic shall be the differences among Judaism, Christianity and Islam. Please feel free to ask me for help; you have three days to prepare." *Now we will see just how blessed he is.*

Nathan frantically thought of ways he could graciously refuse the cantor but there wasn't one. It wouldn't be appropriate to refuse any request from the cantor; leading sechut was expected; it was part of the training.

Three days later with dinner out of the way, David Chechik rose from his chair at the head table and made the announcement.

"I believe Nathan will be leading *sechut* tonight; everyone, please...Nathan?"

Nathan walked to the front of the dinning hall seemingly a little preoccupied. He was a little taller now, only five eight, but for a Roth he was a giant. The late afternoon sun made his dark tan and sandy blond hair shine as he turned and faced his fellow Zionists. He tried to find a place for his hands; deciding on his back pockets, he began his assigned task.

"I have been asked to talk about the differences among Jewish, Christian and Muslim religions. I have chosen to add Hinduism and Buddhism as well. To exclude them would show they weren't worthy or perhaps not as important as other religions. After giving this subject more thought than I really cared to, I found absolutely no differences among them whatsoever."

Nishi swallowed and hoped he'd given Nathan more than he could handle.

"Oh, c'mon, Nathan, you're not serious," said the boy from Montreal sarcastically.

"Maybe you should have given it more thought," said another

David Chechik spoke the loudest. "I don't think Nathan has finished speaking, Chavareem."

"Thank you, Rosh Chechik, I haven't. I believe it is the practices of these religions that are different, not the religions. God does not, in my opinion, care one way or another which religion someone practices, as long as one practices something."

He spoke in phrases and short sentences, articulating which after once heard, seemed so logical and simple.

"Each of these religions share a common resolve; they bring people closer to God. It is only the past and some people's interpretation of past events that causes us to think one religion is different from another."

There were no further interruptions.

"Perhaps if we didn't try to find differences that tend to separate us, the harder we might try to find out that which binds us together. I am certain God created the human being, but I'm equally certain we weren't created for God's entertainment. Is it not foolish to assume that God created different kinds of human beings? We are not Jewish human beings or Christian human beings; we are simply human beings. The God I know had no intention of finding ways to separate that which he had just created. I personally don't care what anyone else believes, and I don't think God does either."

The boy from Windsor called out from the back of the *chadar*, "How can we change that which has been driven into us for the last five thousand years?"

"I know that no one can change the past, and you can't change anything in the future. The only time and place you can change anything is well...right now. I believe that all of us can change, but first we must realize it's possible only to change something in the present." Nathan paused and looked into the eyes of the dozen young Zionists who now sat on the floor in front of him.

"Forget the past, Chavareem, concentrate on today. It's the only time you can change anything."

"This is how you explain things?" shouted the cantor. "This is not an explanation; you have not addressed why. Why do we believe in different religions? This is the question. Explain that!"

Nathan closed his eyes as he listened to the cantor's question and smiled at him before answering.

"Look around you, Cantor," he said. "No one needs an explanation for everything that's beautiful in the world. We don't need an explanation for the mountains and the valleys, or the rivers and lakes, or the flowers or the trees. How egotistical of us to ask God for an explanation for us. God never intended to explain us. If he had, I'm sure it would be as simple and as beautiful as everything else."

Cantor Nishi's heart was still racing as he walked slowly back to his room in the main house. With his gray beard and deep wrinkled face, he looked and walked more like a man in his eighties, not his sixties. He paused at the bottom of the stairs and shook his head deciding it would be best to rest on the back veranda before going up to his room.

How was it possible? Hardly a man and yet his words were those of a teacher; a rabbi but not a rabbi...something more than a rabbi. How could he know these things? It's not possible...the prophecy? No, it couldn't be. The old cantor covered his face with both hands then whispered, "Could it?"

Merriam Weis found him sitting on the top step at the back of the *chadar* and sat down next to him. They could see over the tents and across the lake to the setting sun.

"Nathan." It was barely a whisper. "Nathan, are you always this talkative?" she asked.

Nathan rubbed his eyes and yawned before he noticed her. He thought he was dreaming. His lips parted and appeared as if he was about to say something, but he just stared at her unable to speak. She was so beautiful. She had enormous almond eyes, so dark and yet so alive. Her lips so full and her skin so smooth, he held his gaze and relished in her beauty.

"Everyone wants to talk to you, you know. They're all still in there. I don't think anyone will ever sleep again until you tell them to."

She was joking of course. Maybe if she made him laugh, he might talk to her. She had made earlier attempts to get his attention but he was always too busy to notice her. This was a chance she wasn't going to pass up.

He tried his best not to laugh but it was just too funny. Suddenly the back door to the *chadar* opened.

"Here he is. Here he is!" they shouted to the others inside. Merriam quickly grabbed Nathan's hand as the two of them jumped to the ground and ran down the road towards the lake.

It was way past lights out by the time they started back. Merriam did most of the talking; Nathan was content just looking at her as she became more beautiful every minute. He couldn't take his eyes off her; nothing around him was more pleasing to look at. When he did look away, it was only to ease her concerns.

"You're staring again," she said. "It's a little embarrassing."

She didn't mind really; she liked looking at him too, but it was his mind and the way he spoke to her that intrigued her the most.

"You're not like other boys I know," she said. "You don't say dumb things and try to impress anyone...you just impress everyone. How do you know all those things, Nathan?" she asked. "At nineteen, how do you know so much about life?"

"I don't know, Merriam," he said. "I just know what I think. I don't think about what I know."

"Will I see you tomorrow?" she asked.

"I won't try and stop you."

"Good night, Nathan."

"Good night, Merriam."

That was two weeks ago and every night since Nathan and Merriam had sat together in the moonlight by the lake.

He kissed her forehead, put his arm around her shoulders and held her close to him. He rubbed her back and neck. He stroked her hair and felt the softness of her cheek. She turned and kissed him full on the mouth, their lips gently searching for the perfect place, their tongues moving inside, urging them forward. Her hand found him and rested there, then moving, gently squeezing him through the material that bound him. His hand searched under her white linen shirt and caressed her breast. He held it and marveled in its texture. More desperate now, they tugged and pulled at each other's clothes, struggling to free themselves, believing only their nakedness could satisfy their passion.

"Nathan, Merriam, you there?" The old cantor's voice came from close by, the sudden sound putting an end to what might have been a mistake.

Merriam quickly hid behind the wall of the shvitz.

"Just having a late swim, Cantor. I'll see you on the veranda."

"Right away, Nathan. please," he said.

Ten minutes later they faced each other on the back veranda. The cantor's dark eyes betrayed his anger.

"You might want to think about what you're getting into, Nathan."

"What do mean, Rabbi?" Nathan said.

"I mean your friendship with Merriam Weis."

"What's this?" Nathan said in Yiddish.

"I don't think you realize who Merriam's father is," he said. "And what he would say if he knew you were having your way with his daughter."

"This is not your concern, Rabbi!"

Nathan was angry but wouldn't allow it to overtake him. He fixed his eyes on the cantor.

"It is inappropriate and poor manners to assume I have or would ever take advantage of Miss Weis. Furthermore, we won't let this intrusiveness lessen our mutual respect for one another, will we, Rabbi?"

Nathan didn't wait for a reply; he simply stared into the cantor's black pea-shaped eyes as if telling him to consider carefully what he had just said, then turned away and left the veranda.

Parents Day. One week before the end of camp, the parents were invited to spend a day with the campers. All soon-to-be-graduates had a clear understanding of what it's like to be a Zionist. Their parents came to be impressed with their knowledge of Jewish culture and religion. Only Sam Weis came to see where his money was going, and to talk to Nathan Roth.

Nathan wondered if there was anything more conspicuous than a black stretch limo parked in front of the old house. He could see several men in gray suits standing on the front veranda next to Cantor Nishi and David Chechik. There was another older man with white hair standing next to Merriam. His hand rested on her shoulder as Nathan approached. Suddenly the white haired man moved and blocked his way.

"You Nathan Roth?" he said harshly. It sounded more like an order than a question. "You're the son of Manny Roth, a whoremonger and thief. Do you think I would let the likes of you anywhere near my daughter, you little bastard? If I ever see you again, Roth, it will be at your funeral. Get that vermin out of my sight!"

"Daddy!" Merriam shouted.

"Quiet! I will deal with you later."

Sam Weis motioned to the three oversized men in the gray suits and snapped his fingers twice.

"Let's go, kid, you're already packed."

The tallest one tried to grab Nathan by the collar and push him into the limo. Nathan reached over the arm of his assailant and grabbed the middle fingers of his left hand, ducked underneath and twisted around to the side holding his attacker's fingers backwards, forcing him to his knees. He didn't see the man behind him until it was too late. Nathan dropped to the ground from the blow to the back of his head. Forty minutes later he was thrown from the limo at stop two seventeen.

Chapter Fourteen

Twenty of Canada's finest sat on metal chairs in heavy weight dress uniforms.

"Captain Aaron Roth!"

Aaron wondered if they were being called in reverse order. Being the first to stand in line meant he had to wait for the rest to be called before receiving his commendation. He wouldn't have minded if it wasn't so damn hot—90 degrees and a hundred percent humidity. *Just another perk,* he laughed to himself. Just another example of how ridiculous the Canadian armed forces were. *They spend more time handing out medals than they do handing out combat missions, that's for sure. Why in hell had I become a fighter pilot? It sure wasn't because I wanted to sit on my ass all day filling out flight plans. AFB Gimli, Manitoba—talk about the asshole of the universe.*

Gimli had one gas station and three million flies. A town so unimportant no one had even bothered to give a name to the only paved street. Its only residents were people who provided services to the military and the officers and wives of enlisted men who could afford to live off base. A big night in Gimli was to watch the bulldozers scrape and shovel millions of dead insects off both sides of the street, then drop them into the waiting dump trucks. Add the summer heat and the putrid smell of dead bugs and you'd swear you were in hell.

Aaron had few options; the Canadian military doesn't ask what you want to do for the next three years. They simply look for places for you to hide. There were maybe three ways for a Canadian fighter pilot to see combat: either as part of a joint military task force with the U.S. in defense of their common border, a contingent to fulfill Canada's obligations under a treaty to a foreign country, or through a police action ordered by the Security Council of the United Nations. Canada hadn't sent soldiers into battle since World War II and had refused all requests to do so ever since. That was unless, of course, it wasn't authorized by the government—in other words, special operations. Under Canada's Official Secrets Act, the government didn't have to publicly disclose any military operation crucial to what it deemed "a threat to national security."

The newly appointed head of special-ops was Major General Desiree (Dez) Granville—the same man who had been Aaron's commanding officer for the last two years, and the man who decided to start at the other end of the line handing out medals.

Aaron remained at attention and graciously accepted his medal.

"Well done, Captain," said the general. "Meet me in my office at sixteen hundred. I want to talk to you."

"Yes, sir!"

Aaron was certain the general was going to ask him to prepare some sort of going away party. It wouldn't be the first time he had been asked to organize events for senior staff. He had logged more flight time picking up lobster and liquor from exotic places than anything else. The general called them personal favors. "You'd be doing me and the service a personal favor, Roth." Aaron never refused a personal favor; at least he got to fly, and if he could impress the right people the sooner he and the general could get out of this hellhole.

"The general will be with you in a moment, Captain. He asks that you wait in his office." The sergeant opened the door and motioned for Aaron to sit in one of the chairs facing the general's desk.

"Thank you, Sergeant," General Granville said as he bypassed the two men in the doorway and stood behind his desk.

"Come in, Roth. Close the door, Sergeant, and no interruptions unless it's an emergency, understood?"

"Understood, General."

"Sit down, Roth."

"Thank you, sir."

Aaron removed his cap and sat across from the general.

"You're going to Germany with me, Roth. Not as my aid but as a member of a special-ops team." Aaron never changed expression but he sensed something wonderful just happened. "We need a pilot with your expertise, Roth. I was against it at first but the bottom line, Jew or no Jew, you're the best man for the job."

"A Jew, sir, what..."

"Never mind that now, Roth. Suffice it to say, the Middle East will be our theatre of operations. This is a classified mission, Roth. No phone calls from now on. You are *persona grata* as of this moment, understood?"

"Sir!"

"I will expect to see you on deck at zero six hundred."

The tall, rugged looking leader of special-ops command stood and extended his hand to Aaron. "Welcome aboard, Captain."

Aaron stood at attention and shook the general's hand, saluted, and wondered why General Granville's return salute lacked the usual enthusiasm.

"That will be all, Roth."

It was August 24, 1965.

Sam Weis knew how to get a point across. Nathan was frightened so much that he felt if he had gone back to live with the Sharnofskys it might have put them in danger. He would call them when he got settled. He missed Merriam desperately; he even tried calling her but hung up before saying anything. *It's probably better this way.* Nathan wondered what Sam Weis meant when he called Manny "a whoremonger and a thief." To Nathan, Manny was a lot worse than that.

Having spent what little money he had left on his ticket back to Vancouver, Nathan found a small room in an old house at the foot of Seymour Street. He wouldn't be there long; the sign in front read "Condemned—Do Not Enter." He didn't know where his mother was and he didn't care where his father was. Lizzy was vacationing with her husband in Europe and when he enquired about Aaron, all they would tell him was that he was out of the country.

He slept during the day and wandered the downtown streets searching for something he didn't know existed. He was looking thin and his clothes were starting to look tattered.

The small neon sign in the window said "Jazz." Inside there was only a dark landing with wide stairs leading down to he knew not where.

It was the music that drew him closer to the dimly lit walls where photos of the great jazz musicians of America hung: Louis Armstrong, Miles Davis, Gene Krupa, Earl "Father" Hines and Fats Waller on one side and Sinatra, Torme and Ella Fitzgerald on the other. He sensed they were all looking at him and smiling. He heard recorded music coming from somewhere as he neared the bottom of the stairs.

He could barely see the young man's face; he was a little taller than him with light blond hair and large blue eyes. He wore a black T-shirt with a gold chain around his neck.

"Good evening, sir, you're just in time. Would you like to be close to the stage?" he asked.

Nathan could see the colored lights above the bandstand at the far end.

"Uh, sure, that would be great," he said.

The young blond host pulled out a chair from beneath a round table near the stage and held it for Nathan.

"How's this?"

"This is great, thanks."

The black ebony Hammond sent reflected rays of colored light across his face. A silver rimmed set of drums sat in the center and a stand up bass rested against the back wall. The young blond appeared a minute later.

"Here, I thought you might like something to drink."

"Uh, thanks, but I…"

"Hey, don't worry about it; it's on the house."

The young freckled face drummer walked on to the small raised platform, picked up his sticks and sat down behind the set of drums. He was maybe twenty with red hair and wore a yellow bow tie over a blue tartan shirt. From the other side an enormous black man took the stage and wrapped his huge arms around the bass. Nathan suddenly felt a hand on his back; the blackest man he had ever seen used Nathan's shoulder in order to help him take the step up to the stage.

"Thanks, kid," he said. Nathan watched as the man perched himself behind the black Hammond organ and began to play.

"One-two-three-four."

He had never heard such wonderful music; he didn't know there was music that could make him feel this way. Some of the tunes were familiar, but to watch the organ player's hands floating across the keys, even his mother couldn't have known it was possible. And when he sang in his deep, raspy voice, the notes and phrases brought new meaning to the words. It covered him. His thoughts and emotions were moving in and out of his mind. Each new melody brought new sensations: some sad, some joyous, and some he didn't understand.

Michael Timothy Taylor held on to the corner of the organ and lowered himself from the stage.

"That was the greatest music I have ever heard," Nathan said.

"Why, thank you, young sir."

"I mean, it was more than great; it was, well, it was just more than I can say."

"You are too kind. Are you a musician?" he asked.

"I sang in church when I was young."

"Well then that definitely makes you a musician. Were you in the choir?"

"Well, no, not exactly; I was going to be a cantor, but my father wasn't in favor of it."

"A cantor! You mean the men who chant in ancient Hebrew?"

"Why yes, it's a long way from jazz though."

"Oh, it's not as far away as you think, especially the blues. I bet you could sing jazz real good. Why don't you sing for us later on? I'll show you how. What's your name, son?"

"Nathan, uh, Nathan...Rose."

"Hmm. Nice name. I'm Mike, and this here's Vinny."

"Hiya, Nathan." The bass player grabbed some air with his hand and winked at him.

It was close to two a.m.; Nathan didn't realize clubs stayed open this late. In fact, The Cellar, as it was called, really didn't even open until midnight.

People had filled the place; there wasn't an empty table anywhere. Tall, masculine looking women sat near the back with their dates. Nathan thought most of them must be drunk or simply had bad taste in women. There were young women with old men, young men with old men, and a ménage of wildly dressed characters looking like they had just stepped out of a Rockwell painting.

Nathan stepped up on stage in front of the organ as Mike handed him the microphone.

"Here, you might need this. You ready, Nathan?"

"I guess I'm ready," he said. He knew the song; it was played all the time on the radio.

"Ladies and gentlemen," Mike started the introduction, "please give a warm welcome for Mister Nathan Rose."

There was a smattering of applause as Mike nodded for Nathan to begin.

"*Summer time and the living is easy.*" He sang it slow and soft; the words were rounded and clear. The music followed him as he embraced each note and phrase as if it was being sung for the first time. "*With your mama and papa standing by...*" He held the last note forever; the applause had already started and didn't end until he had handed Mike back the microphone and stepped from the stage. Terry, the blond host/waiter and bouncer, was the first to greet him.

"Man, I just knew there was something about you. I knew it when you walked in; man, can you sing or what?"

"Gee, thanks. I really didn't think I could."

The next night and for each night thereafter, Nathan worked hard on his new passion. He learned a new song every day and sang it the same night.

"You learn a few more and I'll start paying you," Vincent said. You wouldn't have known Vincent was the owner; Nathan didn't know until right then. A couple of weeks later and Nathan received his first paycheck.

Months had passed; a new world had opened up to him. Jazz was all he thought about, jazz and maybe girls. There were several, but none would ever make him forget Merriam.

It was around four when Michael and Nathan sat together at the round table in front of the stage; everyone else had gone except for Terry. The ceiling lights were on and you could see what you never could see earlier. It was just a basement with open beams and joists going a hundred different ways. The stage lights were on and a rainbow of colors covered Michael's face.

Nathan had grown fond of his friend and mentor who was a little overweight with a bad hip, six feet tall, plus the two inches for the afro; he looked a bit like Oscar Peterson. All Nathan really knew about him was that he was married and lived somewhere on the east side. Michael really didn't talk much, but when he did it was always with respect and kindness; but sometimes, he just liked to pull Nathan's leg.

"Well, Nathan, I'll be moving on in a couple of days. Yep, got a pretty good gig in Seattle; godda feed Mama and the kiddies, you know."

"Gee, Michael, that's great. I...I'll miss you."

"Yep, got to do what I got to do; no sense sitting down here when you could be doing something else. Too bad I can't take Vinny; got their own bass you know. Johnny, he's pretty happy; goin' back to Scotland you know. They got no vocal though; don't know what I'm gonna do about that. You know any vocal cats lookin to sing?"

Michael just kept looking up at the ceiling blowing smoke from his Colt and waving at it as hung in the air around him.

"I might know some guy," Nathan said, smiling. "But he's probably too popular now. He'd be pretty hard to pin down for a puny gig in Seattle, but you never know, do ya, Michael?"

There was maybe a couple of seconds of silence before the two of them hollered with laughter.

"You like turkey, Nathan? My Ginny's makin' turkey for dinner. You interested?"

"I am very interested."

Ginny was almost as big as Michael. Her large brown eyes sparkled and matched the color as her skin.

"Ginny, this is Nathan. I asked him to join us for dinner."

Seated in sofas and chairs on every wall, the kiddies, all nine of them, waited quietly to be introduced.

"Now this here is Michael Junior; that's Gregory, and that's William." With each new name came a new smile, no highs or hellos, just smiles, smiles as big as a house.

"And this little bit is Veronica," Ginny said, as she walked in carrying the latest addition to the family.

Nathan looked around the room and looked at each face again.

"I know I won't remember everybody's name," he said, "but it's going to be fun trying. Now, this is Gregory, right?"

"No!" they shouted.

"OK…it's Parish."

"No!" they shouted again.

"OK, OK, this, this…is…"

Nathan walked slowly toward five-year-old William.

"This is…"

Nathan extended his arm and pointed his finger at William's stomach; where upon reaching him, he tickled him on both his sides. "William!" Everyone screamed with laughter; the younger ones pulled Nathan to the ground and desperately tried to tickle him.

Suddenly Ginny clapped her hands and announced, "All right, everyone, wash up for dinner; hurry."

It was tight; everyone sat elbow to elbow, but it felt good to be part of it.

"Nathan," Ginny said, "would you lead us in prayer?"

"Sure, I'd love to."

Ginny had done this to some of Michael's other friends; she loved a good laugh, but this time, no one was laughing. Nathan took Michael Junior's and Ginny's hand as all bowed their heads and waited for Nathan to speak.

"Dear Lord, bless this home and all who live here, for they truly love You. Bless them and guide them through. Keep them safe and keep them close. Hide from them what others do. Dear precious God, it's Your heart we seek, if only this once, the rest will keep. Amen."

"That was..." Ginny's mouth stayed open a little too long, "wonderful."

Nathan, sensing her embarrassment, was quick to change the subject.

"Wow! That is the biggest turkey I've ever seen."

After dinner there was a report on pollution by Michael Junior. Then there was the poem by Robert Frost courtesy of Loretta, and finishing it off was William singing, "When You Wish Upon a Star." Later, Nathan hugged all nine and said good night, promising to visit again.

Michael nodded and appeared lost in thought as the two friends stood looking out over the highway traffic from the back balcony.

"Thank you for the very entertaining evening, Mike. You sure have some great kids there. I guess I'll be going now, Mike; I don't know how late the buses go."

"Uh, oh, yes, the buses, I forgot about the buses. You know, Nathan, you're the first white man that's ever been in this house. I can't believe how my kids like you, and my wife...well she thinks she's died and gone to heaven. You're quite the kid, Nathan. I can't explain it, but there's definitely something different about you, something good, I think."

The following week Michael and Nathan drove the hundred and twenty miles to Seattle's foremost jazz club, The Sky Bar. At the top of Normandy House, it was a far stretch from The Cellar. There were picture windows on every wall and white linen table clothes on each round table placed in a circle five deep around a slightly raised center stage, and separated on all sides by the dance floor. A brand new baby grand stood stately in the center of the stage.

"Not bad, huh, kid?" Michael said.

"No organ?" Nathan asked.

"Not this time. This place is a bit more sophisticated, if you know what I mean. A cup of coffee could break a guy. Let's catch dinner down the block."

The bell over the door was a sure giveaway; this wasn't the most popular restaurant in town. It was long and narrow with a row of red stools at the counter and a row of booths on the other side. One man at the end of the counter was reading a newspaper as Michael and Nathan sat in a booth reading the menu.

"You nigger stupid, boy?" the man said, looking at Nathan. "You take that big nigger outa my café or I'll carve you a new hole."

Nathan began to stand but Michael quickly stopped him.

"Hold on, pal! We don't wanna upset the man. Let's just find somewhere else to eat."

"You're not going to say anything to that ignoramus?"

Michael looked at his young friend with sternness in his eyes.

"Ya leave ignorance where you find it, Nathan; otherwise it will follow you wherever you go."

Michael was his own agent and was seldom without work. He told Nathan just how hard this business could be.

"Sometimes you have no choice where you work kid; you gotta grab onto whatever will keep you working; an artist has to work."

He explained that one day Nathan might get an offer to work with other musicians where he wouldn't be needed, or vice versa. "You try and stay together but sometimes it just doesn't work out. Don't worry, kid, you'll be all right."

It happened quicker than either of them expected.

The Sky Bar was as packed as usual; it didn't take long before people heard about the young singer and his amazing voice. Michael and Nathan had become the hottest duo in town and tonight would mark their first anniversary.

She was big, black and beautiful; he was bigger, blacker and hardly beautiful. They sat at the same table three nights in a row, obviously hotel guests, but then again they were the only black people he had ever seen at the club, except Michael, of course.

"They call me Miss Lovey," she said, leaning over the piano. "I love what you do with a song and I'd love you to come and sing at my place." Nathan didn't know what to make of her.

"I'll have to talk to my piano player," Nathan said. "I think we're booked until January."

"Sure, you do that. Just remember, we have no need for another piano player. I know what you're getting here, kid. So, if you want to make more than double that, show up tomorrow night and we'll discuss the details."

Turned out Miss Lovey wasn't the kind of person who took rejection well; you might say she didn't take it at all. A few years earlier she'd taken advantage of her late husband's connections with the mob and borrowed enough money to open her well-known nightclub. Nathan wasn't sure Miss Lovey was what he needed.

"It's a great opportunity, kid," Michael said. "That Lovey owns the biggest club in the state, and she's real connected. Probably set you up all the way to Vegas. I think you should do it. I'll get by, don't you worry about that; you just remember us little people when you're on top, OK, kid?"

"When I'm on top, you'll be there with me, Michael," he said.

They rehearsed four hours a day, every day, for two weeks. Nathan hadn't had one day of music lessons or any formal training; he had to rely solely on his ear and his sense of timing. The bandleader was patient but demanding as he played the same eight bars over and over again until Nathan finally figured it out.

"You have to be right on, kid," he said. "Right from the start, or the whole thing will sound like shit. Now, try it again."

This wasn't The Cellar or The Sky Bar; there was nothing casual about Lovey's. There was a forty-foot stage with overheads and footlights and a twenty-piece orchestra that sat behind logo music stands with the letter ***L*** on the front. Miss Lovey brought in performers from all over, usually unknown, but a successful two weeks at Lovey's could lead to star billing in Vegas or New York.

The marquee read "Nathan Rose, the boy with the golden voice."

Nathan looked down from the upstairs balcony and over the packed house; ten rows of white linen covered tables surrounded the stage on three sides. Each ringside seat had bouquets of roses with a single red rose on each of the other two hundred tables.

Lovey knew how to promote an act, and the people knew. Known or unknown, Lovey never failed to impress everyone with her ability to showcase new talent.

He was ready, he thought. *Can't turn back now. Nerves or no nerves, it is too late to run away.*

He hadn't had much contact with Miss Lovey; she was seldom around during rehearsal, but as she approached him fifteen minutes before the opening night curtain, he sensed things were about to change.

"Now, I know you're going to wow them, Nathan," she said. "Just remember to relax and have more fun than you've ever had before." She placed her hand on his cheek with her thumb under his chin and kissed him on the lips. Her mouth covered half his face. "Mmm…I'll see you, after the show," she said.

The band had stopped and the last couple had left the dance floor. The overhead lights went dim and darkness began to blanket the house. Nathan walked quickly to the center stage. Only the ringside people could see him as he stood holding his microphone and took his mark a few feet from the edge.

"Ladies and gentlemen!" Lovey's voice rang out over the PA. "Lovey's Theatre Restaurant proudly presents the boy with the golden voice! Mister Nathan Rose!"

The spotlight hit him; he held the microphone with both hands, bowed his head and, without any musical introduction, began to sing.

"Somewhere there's music…" *Slow and haunting.* "How faint the tune…" *Slow, more power.* "Somewhere there's heaven…" *Don't be early.* "How high the moon…" *One-two.* "There is…" A thunder of music hit the audience as Nathan timed it perfectly. The audience applauded as soon as he broke into an up tempo version of the jazz classic.

He took the last note up an octave and sent the audience over the top, and that was only the opening number.

He wore a white tuxedo and a white silk tie with a white cotton shirt. His green eyes sparkled and reflected beams of light back into the eyes of the audience. He dazzled them; he could only see the faces of the people at ringside but everyone in the place felt he was looking directly at them. They loved him and he loved them. He strolled across the stage as if it was his own as people clapped and sang and snapped their fingers. It was nonstop entertainment, and as loud as they had become, they fell completely silent as some even cried during the ballads.

The hour and ten minute show came to an overpowering climax; the music still played the opening theme as Nathan shook the hand of everyone in the front row and left the stage to cries of "More!" and "Encore!"

"Leave 'em wanting more kid," someone once said. He wanted to stay out there; he would have sung all night, but business is business. The ushers had to get everyone out before they could let the late crowd in. Some wanted to stay for the second show but were asked to leave unless, of course, they made it worthwhile. If you had enough money or you were important enough, Lovey made sure you got what you wanted.

After the last show, Nathan's dressing room was full of people, people he didn't know, all trying desperately to talk to him or just wanting to be near him.

"This is the greatest night of my life," one said.

"Please, Nathan, just one picture."

There were at least a dozen invitations to dinner and a barrage of autograph requests.

"I know you're going to be famous one day," the petite blonde said, shoving the pen and program into his hand.

It was past two. Suddenly Lovey walked in without knocking and leaned up against the door she had closed behind her. She didn't say a word; she just stood there watching him. Her breathing got deeper making her breasts rise and fall beneath the low-cut black sequined dress. She reached for the light switch on the wall next to the door and the room went dark except for the small red table lamp on the dresser, which shed enough light to see her coming towards him. She picked him up off his chair with both hands and pulled him to her. Her mouth covered his; her tongue was so deep inside him he could have swallowed it. She was stronger than him; he could hardly move and it was getting harder to breathe. Her lips finally released their grip on his mouth and moved over him kissing and licking his neck and chest as she unbuttoned his shirt and threw it to the floor. Down on her knees, she ran her tongue over his stomach while undoing his belt and opening his zipper, letting his pants fall around his feet. He felt her long nails as she reached for his penis and took it in her mouth.

"Mmm…I love white meat," she said. "You're a good boy, Nathan. You stay that way and I'll take care of you."

He was exhausted. Miss Lovey had had her way with him; there was nowhere on his body that she hadn't kissed, licked or bitten. As she closed the door behind her, Nathan was certain she'd be back for more. It wasn't as if he didn't think she was beautiful, there was just too much of her, or maybe not enough of him—he couldn't decide. What he did decide was not to hang around his dressing room after the show from then on.

He had avoided her for two weeks; it was closing night and Lovey had had enough.

"So, you think I'm pissed at you, don't you, Nathan?" she said, standing over him in his dressing room. "You think I'd let you avoid me if I didn't want you to?"

"Oh, Lovey!" Nathan pleaded. "I was just coming to see you. I wanted to tell you how great you've been to me, and well, here you are."

"Is that so?" she said.

"Yes. In fact, I've had so many offers, I was hoping you could advise me on which way to go; not only that, Lovey, I wanted you to know I haven't told a soul about our night together. I got so carried away. I didn't want to ruin our business relationship with a dumb mistake. I hope you have forgiven me."

She was at a loss for words. Who did this kid think he was kidding anyway? She picked him up and forced him against the dressing room door. Once again her mouth and tongue were hard at work. He tried to move to the side but she wouldn't let go.

He'd had enough. Pushing her head back, he succeeded in finally extricating himself.

"I can't do this!" he shouted.

Grabbing a jacket from the back of the door, Nathan ran out the dressing room, leaving her frustrated and humiliated on the floor.

Two hours later he was blowing kisses as the roses fell around him. It hadn't been planned but ever since the second night the audience had started throwing their roses on stage as he closed the show.

"Good night, Seattle!"

Just walk off stage, turn right, down the three stairs, along the hall, through the kitchen and out the door, and don't stop till you hit L.A. Quickly now, one final wave and I'm at the steps...not too fast...down the hall...good, no one in the kitchen...slightly quicker past the grill to the end and out.

He made it to the heavy metal door, took a deep breath and flipped the bar. Slowly he pushed it open, stepping over the threshold and down a foot to the recently tarred alleyway.

The light that hung from the telephone pole next to the Fiat was broken.

Thank God the car is still there.

Scrapping the key back and forth, he struggled to find the keyhole. He inserted it and opened the driver's door. The Fiat's interior light came on exposing Bruno's face in the side mirror.

"You goin' somewhere, kid? Not even gonna say goodbye?" Nathan turned and faced Lovey's enormous bodyguard. "Gonna have to mess you up now, kid," he said. "Too bad. You're pretty good; maybe in another life."

The big man's hand reached and caught Nathan by the neck, picked him up and threw him over the roof of the car and onto the sticky ground on the other side. Slowly the ruthless giant stocked his prey.

Believing he'd find Nathan lying in wait, Bruno quickly turned back just as Nathan's powerful and accurate kick to the groin dropped the beast to his knees. It must have been instinct; he knew his life was in danger. Frantically, he looked for a weapon, anything to stop the beast from getting up.

Bruno reached for his gun. The empty Jack Daniel's bottle smashed over his head as the .44 Magnum slipped from its holster and fired as it hit the pavement. Nathan saw the hole in the beast's forehead just before he landed face first into a pool of tar.

Chapter Fifteen

"I'll clean up here, kid. You better get moving," he said.

He was standing directly behind the fallen giant with the top end of the Jack Daniel's bottle still in his hand. It happened so fast, there was no time to think. The dark heavyset stranger picked up the fallen pistol. "Beat it, kid," he said. "Forget what you saw. Now, move!"

It was past noon when he decided to pull into the parking lot of the roadside diner. He'd driven all night and still couldn't get the image out of his mind of the beast still lying in the alley and the stranger who miraculously came from nowhere. The police were probably looking for him. He thought of turning himself in and letting the chips fall where they may; on the other hand, he hadn't done anything but defend himself. He hadn't pulled the trigger; it just went off. The stranger said he would clean up; maybe no one would know it ever happened, but what about Lovey? She probably had a dozen other guys on the payroll. If he showed up in Los Angeles they'd probably be waiting for him. She must have known about his next gig; after all, with the publicity he got, everyone knew. He had to think, he had to eat and he had to sleep; maybe some food first, at least it might stop the pain in his stomach.

Nathan walked up the wooden stairs of the diner and took a seat at a table at the far end next to the window. He hadn't noticed the white Cadillac stop on the other side of the highway and the two men who sat in the front seat staring at the diner.

"What'll you have, dear," she said.

She was as big as a house, with a smile to match. She wore a white dress and a red-checkered apron that hung around her neck and tied at the waist.

"You'll never get that tar out, you know, dear. I hope the rental place doesn't make you pay for it."

"Huh?" Nathan looked down the front of his white tuxedo suddenly realizing how ridiculous he must look.

"Must have been a hell of wedding; need some coffee, dear?" The affable waitress held the pot over the table but Nathan refused.

"Uh, no, thanks. Maybe orange juice and some scrambled eggs and toast, please."

"Let's put some sausage on the side," she said. "I think you need some meat on those bones."

He was somewhere in California; he remembered the sign a few miles back on Interstate 5—"Redding, CA." He tried to focus on a plan; somewhere to go, somewhere to hide, but there wasn't anywhere.

"Here you go, dear," she said, placing the plate of food on the table in front of him. "Isn't that your car, dear?"

Nathan looked to his left; there were two tall black men in black suits standing on either side of the Fiat; two more sat in the front seat of a black sedan parked behind blocking any escape.

The front door to the diner opened and a huge black man came in and looked directly at him.

"Back there," the waitress shouted, "through the kitchen!"

Nathan quickly jumped from his chair and headed towards the kitchen. The black-suited man ran after him but was knocked off balance by the waitress plunging him into and over some tables. He tried desperately to get up, throwing tables and chairs out of his path as the waitress pretended to trip and fall, landing backside first on top of him, forcing him to his stomach and making it impossible for him to move.

Outside, Nathan crouched behind a blue pickup; the two beside the Fiat were running towards the diner as the black sedan spun away from the Fiat and headed around the other side. This was his chance. His heart pounding, Nathan made his run to the car. Frantically, he fumbled to find the ignition. He let the clutch out too fast and sent the Fiat spinning out of control across the highway, hitting the back fender of the white Cadillac, stalling the Fiat. He turned the key again and then again trying to restart it; he was done.

"C'mon, baby, don't fail me now!" he pleaded.

The two men were only feet away when the Fiat finally started. He put it in gear and sped south down the highway. The black sedan picked up the other two and chased after him, followed by the white Cadillac.

The Fiat was no match for the powerful sedan; the road was winding up hill and Nathan could tell they were gaining on him. If he could make it to the top of the hill, he might be able to outrun them. He saw them in the rearview mirror; they were right behind him. The white Cadillac drew up next to the sedan with its windows down. The barrel of a shotgun appeared from the passenger side and fired at the driver of the sedan. The driver, minus his arms, slid down and fell hard on the accelerator, sending the sedan into the rear of the Fiat. The force of the hit flipped the Fiat over and sent it spinning on its roof across the highway and into a ten-foot trench.

The black sedan was weaving as its occupants desperately tried to remove the driver from the accelerator. The door of the sedan opened and the armless driver fell out onto the pavement and under the wheels of the slowing Cadillac, allowing the black sedan to make its escape.

The gray-suited driver of the Cadillac withdrew his revolver and stood on the side of the two-lane highway waiting while the other man made his way down into the ditch. Nathan lay unconscious at the bottom. He was bleeding from the ear and his legs were hanging out the window; one of them was obviously broken.

Dust rose thirty feet over the highway as the driver of the white Cadillac waived his arms at the helicopter hovering over the crash site. David Chechik expertly set the bird down and waited while Nathan was placed on a stretcher and secured to the frame.

Chapter Sixteen

A Canadian team of archeologists found it thirty feet below the surface in a hollowed-out chamber that hadn't seen the light of day for almost two thousand years. It was rolled up neatly in a stone box and would stay that way until those who felt disclosure would throw the world into religious chaos had an opportunity to investigate its origin. Now, years later, many were still dealing with authenticity issues; there were still others who wanted to dismiss it out of hand. Of course, no one expected to discover anything like this at the dig. Ancient artifacts were dug up by hundreds of archeologists all over the Middle East. It wasn't that unusual to see a dozen different groups cover an entire hillside searching for that one find that might change history. They had no idea that soon their newest find would change the future.

Chiem Nishi stood next to Nathan and spoke softly into the phone. The room had all the equipment you would expect to find in any hospital intensive care unit, only this room had armed guards at the door and dozens more surrounding the perimeter. They walked the halls day and night as Nathan, his head still bandaged and his right leg suspended in a sling, remained in a coma.

"There's no doubt! He is the one." Cantor Nishi whispered goodbye and replaced the phone back in its cradle.

"Good morning, Cantor."

"Oh! Good morning, my dear." Merriam walked to the side of Nathan's bed and touched his cheek.

"He looks so frail," she said. "I know he's frightened; don't you think he looks frightened, Cantor?"

"No, my child. The doctors say he doesn't know or feel anything."

She bent over and kissed his hand and rubbed her cheek with it. She pulled a chair from the wall and sat next to him placing her head on his chest and closed her eyes to pray.

"Oh, God, please hear my prayers. Only you can save him. Only you can bring him back to us. Please, bring 'The Giver' back. Please, God."

Cantor Nishi stood over her and closed his eyes as well.

The still clouds that hung over the ten-acre estate began to move slowly at first, then faster, moving west away from the morning sun. The guards posted outside held their hands up to feel the wind, but there was no wind. In fact, there was nothing. No sounds of lawn mowers and sprinklers and maintenance people talking to each other. Birds and other animals had lost their voices. There were no shadows or beams of light except the one that suddenly reflected off the second-story window on the west side of the mansion.

Nathan's eyes fluttered and blinked several times before they opened, transfixed on the burning light above. From yellow to red to white, the light continued to brighten. It covered and comforted him. It touched him with a thousand feathered torches. He felt and saw his body rising toward the light; closer and closer, now he reached out to the center of the light and touched the flame. His mouth was dry and he couldn't feel his tongue.

"Water, please. I'd really like some water."

Merriam slowly raised her head. *Have I been dreaming?*

"Nathan! It's me, Merriam. You're awake! Oh, Nathan!"

"Don't cry, Merriam," he said. "Everything will be fine now. Is that water ready, Cantor?"

In the days that followed, Nathan adopted a strict regiment of diet and exercise. He worked hard on his rehabilitation and was uninterested in asking the questions both Merriam and Cantor Nishi were certain he would want answered. Several weeks passed and still Nathan hadn't asked a single question. In the evenings he excused himself from the table to spend the rest of the night reading volumes of books from the mansion's enormous library. He understood how his behavior was affecting Merriam. He still loved her but it was different now.

"There is something I must do, Merriam," he said. "I'm not sure exactly what yet, but I am getting closer to knowing. I cannot become distracted, perhaps later, but not now. I hope you understand."

Sam Weis rolled down the window of the black limousine; over the hill and in the distance he could see the many dormers and turrets that topped the mansion's roofline.

"Not too fast, Danny, please."

"Of course, Mister Weis."

He wasn't in a hurry; he'd been away ever since they brought Nathan to his home. Sam wasn't the kind of man to take anyone's word for anything, even the cantor's, and especially his daughter's, who up to recently had not been serious about anything. But it was far different now. All the doubts, all the stories that he thought were a hoax and a fairy tale were true. Six weeks studying and listening to the experts decipher and interpret the scroll had made it clear. The scroll was genuine. He was convinced he would find a flaw, something that contradicted what Merriam and the cantor believed. He had to be sure and now he was. Nathan was "The Giver." Everything he had learned, everything he now knew about Nathan Roth made it undeniable.

In a sense Sam couldn't wait to tell him; in another he felt ashamed knowing he had made such a terrible mistake. He wouldn't blame Nathan if he told all of them to go to hell. My God, he'd sent him into the abyss and it almost killed him. His daughter told him she hated him and would never forgive him. He was one of the wealthiest men in the world but no amount of money would ever be enough to replace what he had almost destroyed.

Sam's black limo moved through the opened iron gates and around the center fountain and stopped. Two men in gray suits stood on either side of the stone lions that guarded the entrance.

More than anxious to hear what Sam had found out, David Chechik hurried down the stairs of the coach house and greeted the limo as it entered the courtyard. There was no point in disclosing anything to Nathan until Sam's return. He thought it strange that Nathan didn't seem to care. Nathan was solely focused on regaining his strength and, for the most part, uninterested in Merriam's requests for intimacy.

What should have taken at least six weeks of therapy, Nathan did in three. He swam lengths in the indoor pool and lifted weights for hours every day. He had evolved, not so much physically, although in excellent condition, there was now a presence about him—a presence David, Merriam and Cantor Nishi couldn't help but notice.

He was in the pool when David told him of Sam's arrival

"He wants to see you, Nathan," he said

"Yes, I'll be right there, David."

The library was massive. Dark mahogany paneled walls shelving thousands of leather bound books rose twenty feet before a cantilevered balcony with brass railings separated the rest of the room from the higher dome that narrowed and framed the stained-glass ceiling.

Sam walked out from behind the black walnut desk and extended his hand as the gray-suited guard closed the double doors behind him.

"I must say you look a lot better than the last time I saw you."

Nathan had really never looked at Sam Weis before; their first meeting wasn't what you'd call cordial. He remembered an angry and violent man, a man willing to do anything short of killing him just to make a point. He saw a different man now, definitely not angry, and as he looked into his eyes he sensed a tenderness in them, almost pleading.

"Hello, Mister Weis," he said, as he took Sam's hand.

"Please, Nathan, sit down."

Sam Weis hadn't apologized for anything in his life. He had always been ruthless and unfeeling, driven to take back everything the Nazis had taken from him. His father died leaving him enough to start his own business, and before his twenty-fifth birthday he became Germany's youngest merchant banker. By the fall of 1938 the Nazis had seized all his assets and cancelled every financial obligation. Fortunately, he had already made investments overseas; without them, he would never have been able to buy his way out. Almost thirty years later, Sam Weis discreetly ran the largest independent merchant bank in the world, financing hundreds of enterprises from oil tankers to airliners and, more recently, bullets to bombs. Sam Weis had become Israel's most powerful financier and facilitator, building unshakeable relationships with the U.S. in support of Israel's right to exist.

It was David Ben Gurion, Israel's first president. who introduced him to Merriam's mother, Sarah. She was half his age, a sabra who, like so many others, had lost her parents to an Arab raid on her home near the Syrian border. She was beautiful and passionate; their one night together was all they had. When the pregnancy was announced, and as much as he pleaded with her, Sarah would not leave her beloved Israel—not for him and not for her unborn child. Tragically, Sarah died giving birth, and immediately Sam flew back to Israel and brought Merriam home to Toronto. She was dark skinned, with enormous almond-shaped eyes and as beautiful as anything Sam had ever seen. Unfortunately, Sam had little experience with children; he regretted not being the kind of father he now wished he'd been. He loved her, but until now never knew how to express it. He'd never been religious in the Biblical sense; that was before. Now he sat across from the one person, the only person, who after more than two thousand years had come with a message that could change the world forever.

They sat in the two high-backed leather chairs in front of the fireplace; the flames crackled and sent flickering yellow light across their faces. Nathan could easily see Sam's hand shake as he reached for a cigarette and lit it. He took a long drag, exhaling slowly, and tried to gather himself.

"I'm sorry, Nathan. I'm sorry for so many things; I don't know where to begin."

"It's all right, Sam, I know everything."

"I don't understand; how could you know?"

"It's not important how I know, Sam. The important thing is that there is something I must do; I think you know what that is. I'm hopeful you will assist me."

"Is this the prophecy, Nathan?"

Nathan closed his eyes and sat in silence for a minute before speaking.

"I cannot tell you, Sam. I cannot explain what or why God has chosen me—if it is God. I only know that there is much I must do, and I must do it before it is too late. Will you help me, Sam? I need to know that you are willing to give me everything I may need, including your trust."

"I will, Nathan. I will do all that you ask of me."

Nathan stood and felt Sam's tears as they embraced.

For several more hours they talked of the pending military conflict that threatened to destroy Israel and take the world to the brink of another world war, one that may destroy all mankind. Nathan wanted to know the names of each Israeli advocate of peace. He wanted to know the names of any potential Arab ally as well as the most outspoken enemies. He had already read every book in Sam's library on Arab culture and religion. He had put to memory many Arabic idioms and phrases and felt confident that if he heard the language spoken, he'd understand it. He wanted Sam to arrange appointments with every political leader in the region and made it clear that he expected Sam and all who worked for him to do exactly what Nathan told them, including David Chechik, who he wanted by his side at all times. Sam and Cantor Nishi would go on ahead and make all the necessary arrangements; Nathan and David would follow a few days later.

"No one can know exactly where or when I arrive in Israel, Sam," he said. "There are some who will do anything to stop what we are about to do."

It was February 15, 1967.

Chapter Seventeen

It had been five years since the story first appeared in the tabloids. Even the least recognized archeological magazines didn't play it up as an important historical find. A couple of religious periodicals reported it, but Israel had prohibited anyone from even looking at the scroll, never mind studying it. It would take the most important man in the Zionist movement to unearth and expose to the world that which had remained a secret for two thousand years.

It was in the form of a letter; it was written to a long list of students by a young rabbi named Jesus Ben Joseph and sealed in a stone box. According to the experts, every component of the find dated back to the Resurrection. The document predicted every political change and rebellion that had happened or was about to happen. It spoke about the Roman occupation and their threat to prosecute the young rabbi for preaching rebellion. One night, God had spoken to him in a dream and told him of the prophecy.

A *young man shall come and set right that which had turned the hearts and minds of man. He will come from the other side of the world. He will be one month and eight days short of his twenty-first birthday. He will be the youngest of three bastard children. The son of the proselyte Mary, he will be both Christian and Jew and speak every language. He will sing to God and God will hear him. He will come to free the imprisoned and they will be let go. He will find friends among his enemies and enemies among his friends. He will gather the masses in God's name and put an end to war, war of every kind. He will take the blame and ask forgiveness so others will know his power. He will bring joy to those who have never known it and make simple all that is complicated and uncover all that is hidden. He will cut the bonds of the past and open the door to the present. His name is Nathan. He will be called "The Giver."*

Refueling at a private airport outside of Belfast, David Chechik was deep in thought as Nathan slept in the seat next to him. The converted 707 would be at their disposal for as long as they needed it.

David was seventeen when he and his parents first landed in Israel. His mother and father were teachers at the university before the Nazis threw them out of their home. With only the clothes on their backs, Joseph and Ruth Chechik took their son through the back streets of Prague, avoiding the Gestapo, and escaped to Switzerland. During the war his parents had been a part of the Jewish underground, each day putting their lives in danger as they led small groups of refugees through mountain passes and frozen fields to freedom. Making their way to Israel in 1946, Joseph and Ruth were welcomed as heroes and patriots and immediately asked to help in forming Israel's first government. By Independence Day in 1948, Joseph Chechik had become a very important man, accepting the position as Israel's representative at the United Nations.

It was the summer of 1956; David had returned to New York after completing his pilot training and was looking forward to spending time with his beloved parents. Ambassador Chechik, Ruth and David, looking every bit the soldier in his dress uniform, were approached by a large group of reporters in front of the United Nations building.

"Is it true, Mister Ambassador, does Israel have the bomb?" one reporter shouted above the others.

Joseph was as always articulate and direct. "The security of Israel is our foremost concern; we will continue to plead with our Arab neighbors to allow us to live in freedom and without fear. We..."

The single rifle shot fired from the hotel window across the street passed through Joseph's neck and into Ruth's temple, as David was thrown to the ground in the melee. By the time he turned to find them, Joseph and Ruth Chechik lay dead in the street.

David blamed the United States for his parents' deaths but refused to return to Israel. Instead, he applied for immigrant status to Canada. He'd had enough; his parents were dead because of their passion and commitment to Israel. He never wanted to see Israel again. He chose Canada because it was safe; it had no enemies on its borders. It was a country where people walked freely without the fear of being shot down on their way to work or blown up as they sit having dinner in a restaurant. The only thing he missed was flying, and when the opportunity to fly rescue for the Toronto fire department came up, he thought he had found the perfect job. That was until he crashed during a rescue attempt, killing his co-pilot and a five-year-old child he had just lifted from a burning car. Recovering in the hospital, he met Cantor Nishi, who introduced him to Sam, who got him the job at the camp. Now he was on his way back to Israel, not as a soldier but as bodyguard to the one they call "The Giver."

He liked Nathan but he was disappointed when he wasn't included in the planning of the mission. In fact, all he knew was that he was to protect him no matter what. He knew of the prophecy but he was not convinced that Nathan held the answer to peace between Arabs and Jews. After all, he hadn't even been to Israel. How could a kid know how to put an end to hatred—hatred that was ingrained into the hearts and minds of Arabs and Jews for the last thousand years?

Ben-Gurion Airport was as busy as any other international airport. Filtering their way through the crowd, Nathan and David and four men in gray suits made their way outside the terminal and hailed two cabs. Sam wanted to send a limo but Nathan thought it too conspicuous. David and Nathan were in one cab in front and the other with the four gray suits followed behind. It was a thirty-minute drive to the hotel.

It was just after three in the afternoon and it not unusual to see a blue and white school bus on the road.

"Why are you slowing down?" David asked the driver.

"The school bus is slowing, sir, not me," he said.

David turned and looked out the back; the second cab was no longer behind them. A white Mercedes with four men inside pulled along side on the left, forcing their cab onto the shoulder. The white and blue school bus came to a full stop; they were boxed in. Their only chance for escape was out the other side. It was too late; the back passenger door opened and Nathan was dragged out and thrown to the ground. David reached for his revolver; the cab driver fired first. Blood from David's head splattered across the window behind him.

The terrorist drove the heel of his heavy boot into the back of Nathan's neck, forcing his face into the roadside gravel. Nathan heard a barrage of gunfire coming from somewhere back down the highway. He tried turning to the left to see David's dead body lying in the back of the taxi. The masked gunman pushed his heel harder into the back of his head as another shouted, "Be careful, you fool! He is no good to us dead!" A black cloth sack was tied around his head and his hands were bound behind his back before he was picked up off the ground and dragged up the steps and pushed to the floor at the back of the school bus. The entire attack had taken less than a minute. It had been well planned by someone, but who? No one was supposed to know who he was. No one was supposed to know anything. He tried to think but the pain in his side made it impossible. He sat on the floor in the center aisle absorbing every bump and hole on the road for hours until the bus finally stopped. A few minutes later the door of the bus opened and Nathan listened to the many voices speaking Arabic, all seemingly happy about their success. Still wearing the black sack over his head, Nathan was pulled from the bus and dragged fifty feet across the gravel courtyard to an abandoned clay building and forced down a narrow flight of stairs, then thrown to the ground at the bottom.

A young but angry voice shouted at him, "Sit, Jew pig! If you move, I will kill you!"

Chapter Eighteen

There were Israeli police everywhere. Sam Weis stood in the center of the King David Hotel lobby surrounded by a dozen uniformed officers while he shouted at an Israeli general. It had been less than an hour since the report came in of the roadside massacre. Five Canadians and one masked Israeli were dead, and no sign of Nathan Roth.

"Mister Weis," the general interrupted. "We have every road and highway covered." The general never let his emotions cloud or interfere with the task at hand.

"We'll find them; don't worry."

"Don't worry! General, are you crazy? You don't know who he is and you tell me don't worry! General, if you don't find him, and I mean fast, the world will collapse and all the 'don't worries' won't mean a thing."

"I understand you care for this man, but the world, sir? I mean, well, that's not really true now, is it?" The general's calm voice did little to alleviate Sam's growing fear.

"General, you don't understand, Nathan Roth is the one! 'The Giver.'"

Everyone in the lobby heard it, especially the reporters.

"Who? You mean Nathan Roth?" The question hung in the sudden silence.

"Who is Nathan Roth exactly, Mister Weis?"

"Who is, or what is 'The Giver'?"

"Isn't that a prophecy?" another reporter shouted.

By morning Nathan's picture appeared on the cover of every tabloid and major newspaper in every corner of the world. The fact that Nathan had been kidnapped made the story even more sensational as well as credible. Soon scholars and religious leaders were being interviewed and asked if they had known of the scroll and of the prophecy. None would admit they were unaware of its existence, especially after Israel allowed the ancient scroll and its contents to be photographed as it lay open on a gold base inside a glass case at the National Museum.

Nathan sat uncomfortably against the basement wall with his hands bound in front of him; the sack over his head had been replaced with a piece of old cloth wrapped around his eyes and tied at the back. It was hard to breath; the stale air that hung around him stunk of urine and something else he didn't recognize. The pain in his side wasn't as bad as the pain in his limbs from sitting on the hard earth for three days. His captor never spoke to him except when he shoved a piece of bread or a can of water at him, saying, "Eat, Jew pig," or "Drink, Jew pig." Nathan wondered if that was all the English he knew.

Mohamed Alzeer sat on the other side of the ten by ten foot basement room tossing pebbles at his prisoner.

"Owe! Your aim is getting much better," Nathan said in Arabic. "Have you thought of trying out for the big leagues?"

"Shut up, Jew!"

He wasn't at all happy with having to stay hidden in the basement; he felt no better off than his prisoner. But to be a freedom fighter meant he did whatever was asked of him. The problem for Mohamed was that he never felt comfortable, knowing if he didn't, he might as well be the enemy. He was told not to take his eyes off him. If the prisoner dies then he dies; it was that simple.

Nathan was jolted by the sudden removal of the blindfold.

"I want to see your eyes when you die," he said in perfect English.

"And I want to see your eyes when I die, too. Thanks."

Nathan looked at his captor for the first time. He was young, about his age, maybe a little taller, with long curly hair and big round eyes. He looked more like a model in a magazine than a terrorist.

"Have you killed many people?" Nathan asked.

"I'd worry about you, Jew pig."

"I'm more worried about you," he said.

"You shouldn't. If it were up to me, you'd be dead already."

"Well at least if I were dead, both of us could leave this place."

The handsome Arab turned his head before Nathan saw him smile. No one spoke again for the rest of the day.

"Good morning, Mohamed. I trust you slept well," Nathan said, as the young Arab woke to the narrow beam of light that flashed across his face.

"How do you know my name?" he asked.

"You call it out sometimes in your sleep—I just guessed, really."

The young Arab placed his rifle on the ground and brought his knees to his chest and closed his eyes. He was only nineteen, the son of a carpenter forced from his home by the Israeli occupation. His mother had been a teacher and, in spite of the difficulties imposed on Arab women, managed to raise her son and two daughters without the usual abuse handed out by insensitive Muslim husbands. His father, Doran, was kind to her and respected her intelligence. He allowed her to teach the children English as long as she made sure they never spoke it in front of anyone they didn't know. It was Doran's older brother, Kareem, once an officer in Nasser's army, who insisted Mohamed join in the fight against Israel. "He will kill many Jews!" he proclaimed.

Mohamed wanted to go to the university but that would never happen now. He was a terrorist and now that he had kidnapped "The Giver," he was certain to die a terrorist.

"How did you learn English, Mohamed?"

"I thought I told you to shut up."

"I know you did, but you telling me is more fun than just sitting here, don't you think?"

This time the handsome Arab couldn't hide his smile and neither could Nathan. They looked at each other and started laughing. Mohamed tried desperately but every time Nathan looked back at him, he laughed louder and louder. Nathan's laugh was so infectious that the young Arab reached over and covered Nathan's mouth with his hand.

It was a gentle hand, soft and comforting. Suddenly both were silent as Nathan placed his hand on Mohamed's shoulder, bowed his head and whispered, "Oh, merciful God, hear the laughter in our hearts. See the joy on our faces. Loosen the bonds of fear. Though our minds are filled with hatred, we seek love everlasting. Oh, gentle Father, this man is mine. Bless all who love him. Take not a single breath before you do; this cannot wait till another time."

Three more weeks passed; Mohamed no longer threw pebbles or shouted obscenities at him. Instead, he talked to Nathan like a friend and brother. He told him of his dream to go to university and how his mother had cried when his uncle made him leave his house and join his fellow terrorists. They talked for hours about his father and mother. Nathan only listened, never judged, and never argued. His eyes shut, fighting off the tears of sorrow, as Mohamed told him how they had lost their home to an Israeli settlement, and how his own people had abandoned them, leaving them without a country. Their only option was to fight the Jews. Mostly the Jews came from Europe, millions of them. Now it was up to a handful of Arabs to take back what had been lost and do whatever it took to send the Jews back into the sea.

Nathan sat quietly looking at the sleeping Mohamed. His gentle look and even breathing took Nathan away from this place as he thought of his family. *Hold my mother close to you, God; never take your eyes from her.* He thought of the monster that had tormented and abused him. *Lead him out of the darkness; tear from his heart the demons that bind him. If only for a moment, let him feel your forgiveness as I do. Guide my brother; make him a safe path to follow. Give my sister a happy life; this is all she needs. I love you, Bubba.*

Nathan slept and dreamt of joy.

"Will you forgive me when they kill you, Nathan?" he asked, as they sat sharing their morning meal.

"Yes I will, my handsome friend. I already have. My only hope is that your family is safe and that they and you will have the joy you all deserve—as it was intended."

The young Arab looked at him quizzically.

"What do you mean, intended, Nathan?"

"Why, it's the gift, my young friend."

"What gift, Nathan?"

"Why, it's the gift that can only be felt when it is given: the gift of joy, the gift of forgiveness. Violence and hatred only bring pain and sadness; there is no joy in that. There is no joy in killing anything. Only those who are locked in the past think that there is joy in those places. Joy can only be experienced in the present; hatred and fear live in our thoughts of the past and the future. You can't feel anything in places that don't exist and you can't change anything in those places, either. God intended us to experience the joy now; he didn't intend for us to explain that which we cannot see or touch. There is no joy in taking anything, Mohamed. When you take a life you give away your joy. The gift of joy is held in each of our hands; when we give it to another, we can feel its power. When we seek to forgive, we throw away the past and the future. It's the gift, Mohamed, and I give it to you, with all my heart."

Mohamed knelt in front of his prisoner and wept.

"Hold me, Nathan, please hold me. I'm so frightened."

Nathan put his arms around his friend and held his head to his chest.

"It's true," Mohamed whispered, "you are 'The Giver.'"

Suddenly their embrace was broken as the door to the upstairs banged against the wall. Two men waited outside while two others came running down the stairs. Mohamed jumped from the floor as Nathan put his hands behind his back.

"Take him! His time is up!" Kareem Alzeer pulled Nathan to his feet.

"Wait, uncle!" Mohamed shouted.

"Quiet! There is no time."

"You don't understand, uncle. He is not our enemy…he is blessed; we cannot…"

Mohamed's uncle struck him across his face "Go! Or die with the Jew," he said, pushing both Nathan and Mohamed up the stairs.

Outside in the courtyard, hidden Israeli soldiers waited for the right moment.

"Hold your fire until Nathan is out of the way," whispered the Israeli general.

They had the entire compound surrounded. The white Mercedes was parked next to the house of clay. Four other small houses on either side, abandoned years ago, provided enough cover to those waiting inside. Two armed terrorists stood by the Mercedes smoking, their rifles strapped casually over their shoulders.

Mohamed followed the first gunman and covered his eyes from the sun as he reached the doorway and stepped out on to the gravel courtyard.

The first shot hit the first exiting gunman in the shoulder, spinning him backwards and to Nathan's right. Another shot ricocheted off the wall and hit Mohamed in the chest, dropping him to the ground.

"No!" Nathan screamed, and fell over his friend. Several more shots and the two smokers were dead. The third terrorist tried to retreat down the stairs but was killed before reaching the bottom.

"This one is still breathing," said a young Israeli lieutenant kneeling over Mohamed. Nathan turned Mohamed on to his back and put his hand over the bleeding wound.

"It's OK! Mohamed, you're safe now. You're going to be all right."

Another Israeli soldier tried to drag the young Arab out from under him.

"Stop! Can't you see he's hurt? Get a doctor over here at once!" Nathan looked up and saw the general standing over him. "Are you in charge here?" Nathan asked.

"Yes, I'm…"

"I don't care who you are! Get this man to a hospital! He is my friend; if anything happens to him, I will hold you responsible. Do you understand me?"

"Yes, Giver, I understand."

"Nathan." Mohamed's voice was growing weaker. "Take me home, Nathan, please. I want to see my mother before I die."

"You're not going to die, my young friend."

The wound was high on the shoulder and not nearly as bad as first feared.

"We will need to take him in for questioning," the young Israeli said.

"You will take him where I tell you to take him. Now help me carry him."

Chapter Nineteen

Israel's foremost financier was making it clear. "You will do exactly what 'The Giver' tells you. Is that clear, General?"

"Yes, Mister Weis, it's clear. But you understand, I only take orders from the prime minister."

"You call him then! He'll tell you the same thing, now do it!"

General Moesha Tosker never felt threatened in his life. The devoutly religious man was a confidant to the prime minister and the chief of staff of the Israeli armed forces. The fact that Sam Weis was barking out orders had little affect on him.

"I have already spoken to him, Mister Weis, and everything will be done as you wish."

Sam still wasn't satisfied.

"Well, where is he? When can I see him?"

"As per your instructions, Mister Weis, I am following a direct order from 'The Giver.' He has ordered me to tell you where he is, but that you are to agree not to contact him. He will contact you when he believes the time is right. He trusts that he can still count on your complete cooperation and that you'll follow his instructions. He also asked that my office and airport staff keep the plane fueled and ready, and to inform you immediately of any changes. Now if you'll excuse me, sir, I have many other things to attend to."

It was not that the general was taking this situation lightly, he wasn't. In fact, he'd hoped the young Canadian was genuine. It would be up to him to make happen what the prophecy predicted. There was nothing he, as general, could do except keep a watchful eye on Israel's borders.

The military ambulance avoided the crowd outside the two-story sandstone building and stopped. Mohamed's mother and father stood at the rear of the ambulance as the young Arab's stretcher was placed in front of them. Nathan stood on the other side holding Mohamed's hand.

"You animals!" Missus Alzeer shouted. "What have you done to my son?"

Mohamed rubbed his eyes with his left hand, trying to adjust to the sunlight. Missus Alzeer, thinking Nathan was in charge, walked around the stretcher and slapped him across the face.

"Murderer, you tried to kill my son!"

"No, Mama! He saved me. He is my friend. He's 'The Giver.' I love him."

Missus Alzeer looked again into the gentle green eyes of "The Giver." The throng of people suddenly went silent as she put her head on Nathan's chest and wept.

The crowd outside the Alzeer home wasn't at all comfortable with the presence of Israeli soldiers, and although many in the street heard Mohamed refer to Nathan as "The Giver," not all were ready to embrace him. That was until Missus Alzeer, aware of how the crowd was beginning to express their hatred for the Jew, stood on a wooden crate and faced them.

"Listen to me!" she said. "My son is safe because of this man. All of us might very well be safe because of him. He is welcome in my home."

She pointed and shook her finger at one man in particular.

"He shall not be harmed by anyone! Do you understand me?"

The man didn't change his expression; he just turned and walked away.

"Come, Father," she said. "Our son is home and we have one more for dinner."

Night fell over Hebron. Nathan slept on a small cot next to his friend. On the morning of the third day, Nathan opened his eyes and watched Missus Alzeer place the tray of tea and pastry on the small round table next to him.

"Where is Mohamed, Mother?" he said in perfect Arabic.

"He is waiting for you outside; eat now, you must be starving."

Missus Alzeer was nobody's fool. She already had a reputation in the neighborhood for being an unruly wife; her husband had been advised by many that he wasn't beating her often enough. Mohamed told her about their ordeal in the desert prison and how he came to believe in the young Jew from Canada. Missus Alzeer saw the pictures and read the articles in the western papers. She had wiped the perspiration from "The Giver's" forehead and in the evenings watched him as he slept next to her son. Her brother-in-law was dead but she did not mourn him. He would have killed Nathan and probably Mohamed as well.

Mohamed loves him. I shall love him too.

Nathan found him outside sitting in a folding chair talking to his father.

"Master, you're awake!"

The handsome young Arab rose and put his good hand on his father's shoulder.

"This is my father, Doran."

Nathan extended his hand but Doran quickly held Nathan's shoulders and looked into his eyes.

"You saved my son. My life and everything I have is yours."

Doran took Nathan's hand and placed the other around his neck and kissed him on both cheeks.

The three companions walked Hebron's crowded streets of stone and earth. Soon there were many, mostly women and children, all trying to get a better look at the one they call "The Giver."

"This is the oldest mosque in Palestine," Doran said. "We should move on."

"I want to look inside," Nathan said excitedly.

His step quickened as he approached the sacred place. All of a sudden an old man fell to the ground in front of him, stopping him before he placed his foot on the first step.

"You are unclean! You cannot be here!" he shouted. Doran reached for the old man and tried to move him away.

"It's OK, Doran. I shall not enter this holy place." Nathan knelt down next to the old man who lay at his feet. "You are a river too wide to cross, old man. You are a mountain too high to climb. I shall not attempt it." Nathan placed his hand on the old man's head. "Come, let's talk awhile," he said.

Nathan sat on the steps of the ancient mosque and talked with him. He listened as the old man told him of his crippled wife and his lost children. He told him of how he had lost everything because of the Israeli occupation; he heard stories of hatred and fear and of how all his people had struggled for freedom from oppression. With nothing left, they took up arms against Israel.

Soon there were hundreds of people in front of the old mosque; they sat cross–legged, watching and listening. Many placed food and drink on the steps before him. His perfect words, spoken in perfect Arabic, entered the hearts and minds of the gathering.

"Oh loving God, a word with You I seek. There are many here who ask of Thee for thousands more a place to keep. It's close but too far away for most to see. You know its name, its time and place; it makes us sing and laugh; it puts a smile on our faces.

"I feel You hide and blind Yourself to those of us who cannot find what lies ahead or far behind. I know You care but times too few You've made it clear why or when or what to do. You've heard me sing of this before. Is it this you want to hear some more?"

Nathan smiled and laughed with them; his words comforted them and joy filled the square.

"Oh precious God, bring summer rain to clear away the tears of time. Let no one catch a cold or flu or hear a cough or achoo!"

More laughter filled the open area in front of the ancient mosque. Nathan waited until the crowd fell silent, bowed his head and prayed.

"Oh Lord, thank You for the laughter; thank You for the joy we feel today. Bless this holy place and my friend Ahmed," he said, placing his hand on the old man's shoulder. "Bless all here who love You. Bless each one, Jew and Arab; we pray You see no difference between us. Amen."

General Tosker stood hidden in the alley next to the mosque. He had heard every word and saw what his eyes thought he would never see, a Jew laughing and rejoicing in the streets of the West Bank. An amazing fellow, he thought. First he throws himself over the body of the man who was going to kill him, and now he speaks to hundreds of Arabs as if they were his brothers and sisters. The general was anxious to report this to the prime minister. *Maybe there is more to this young Canadian than the prime minister thinks.*

In the weeks that followed, Nathan and "The Giver" articles covered the headlines.

"ARE WE READY?"

"NO MORE WAR…EVER?"

"HE IS AMONGST US"

"'THE GIVER' IS HERE!"

It was March 10, 1967.

Chapter Twenty

General Granville had just hung up the phone. He knew there was going to be trouble. He knew there would be something about Captain Roth that would make his job more difficult. He had never figured it would be this difficult. The morning paper on his large metal desk had lain in front of him all day. He hadn't read anything other than the front page. "*NO WAR EVER*!" How could anybody believe such nonsense?"

Aaron was still puzzled and amazed. His kid brother suddenly appearing on the front page of the Berlin newspaper, it was something he couldn't come close to understanding. He had only been back a week since coming out of deep cover. He called and spoke to his mother only yesterday. She said she didn't believe it, and neither did he. Only there he was, right there in the *Los Angeles Times*.

"It's him, isn't it, Mom?" he said. They were looking at the same photograph at the same time.

"Yes, it's him, but how could it be?"

"I don't know, Mom, but I've been ordered to report to the general's office tomorrow morning. I'm sure it's about Nathan."

"He's here, General," announced the aid.

"Show him in, Sergeant," he said without looking up.

Aaron took a seat in front of his commanding officer.

"Let me make this clear, Roth. I didn't want you in the first place, and now this."

"General Granville, sir, I also know nothing about this. I haven't seen my brother in five years; the last I heard, he was singing in nightclubs."

"Well he's singing now, isn't he? Well, look, Roth," he handed Aaron a large manila envelope, "these are sealed orders. Do not open them until zero nine hundred tomorrow; is that clear?"

"Yes, sir!"

"As well, you're to report to UNAFB Bahrain by twelve hundred hours the day after tomorrow. You arrange transport; just confirm flight plan before you leave. That's all, Roth."

Nathan sat in the shade next to his friend and placed the leather-bound copy of the Koran on the wooden table and sighed.

"What's wrong, Master? You don't seem pleased?"

"Oh, Mohamed, will you please stop calling me master! I've asked you a hundred times."

"I'm sorry, Nathan, it just feels so natural. Have you seen the truth in the Koran, Nathan?"

"There is much that is beautiful," he said, "but there is much that should never have been written."

Nathan had spoken many more times since the talk on the steps of the ancient mosque. People from all over the West Bank had come to see and hear "The Giver." They stood and waited outside the Alzeer home in large groups. Sometimes he just walked among them shaking hands and kissing cheeks without speaking. Other times he had casual conversations and still other times he spoke to hundreds as they sat on the ground before him.

He had lived among the Palestinians for three weeks; the street in front of the house had been blocked off and turned into an open-air theatre. Today would be the last time Nathan would speak in the streets of Hebron. Photographers and reporters were everywhere, outnumbering the locals two to one. Nathan via Sam had invited them, disclosing his exact whereabouts for the first time since he had arrived in Israel. All the arrangements had been made; Sam never even considered not following through, and the plane was waiting and ready for the trip to Saudi Arabia.

Nathan raised his hand and quieted the murmuring crowd. He spoke Arabic as if he'd spoken it all his life. His dark tanned face and hands and the traditional Arab clothing he wore gave reason to suspect he had formed an alliance with the Palestinians.

"There are promises to keep!" he proclaimed loudly. "The promises I have given to all who love freedom. I shall seek to fulfill each one of them. I shall face those who would deny us our freedom. I will tell them of the joy that awaits them when they give all they possess to the power of the gift. They shall experience life as it was intended—to love God in their own way, in any and all ways. I shall bend the bars of prisons and set free all who suffer there.

I shall untie the ropes that bind us to the past and open the doors to forgiveness. I will make clear that which was unclear. I shall uncover that which was hidden and place a pillow of peace at the feet of the enemies of peace. I shall replace fear with friendship and hatred with happiness. I shall feel the lips of joy upon my cheek and kiss away the tears of time." Nathan raised his arms over his head, turned his palms upward to the sky bowed his head and prayed.

"Oh mighty God, bless this place and all who gather here. My journey has begun. I cannot wait another day. I shall not waiver in my resolve. I shall not compromise Your trust in me. I feel Your strength in me, oh Lord. Blessed are those who wait for 'The Giver.'"

Chapter Twenty-one

Nathan's words to the Palestinians over the last three weeks had made Sam's job a lot easier. He had been swamped with requests; everybody wanted to meet "The Giver." Every nation, every political entity in the Middle East had not only agreed to a meeting, but had offered everything from citizenship to a royal wedding.

Faisal Ibn Abdul Aziz al-Saud, the most powerful man in the Muslim world, was first on Nathan's list. Nathan believed the Saudi ruler held the key to the rest of the Arab world. If he could persuade the king to believe in him, he could persuade all of Islam.

The 707 jetliner was circling the airport for the third time. Nathan could see people being pushed back off the runway from his window.

"This is the captain, sir. We've been cleared to land; we'll be on the ground in just a few minutes."

Mohamed sat frozen in the seat next to him, his hands gripping tightly to the armrests.

"It's OK, Mohamed, we'll be on the ground soon, and you're not going to die, so try to relax."

Mohamed had made it clear he didn't want to fly. He was thrilled when Nathan asked him to come but when he told him they were flying to Saudi Arabia, it was all Nathan could do just to get him on the plane.

Sam's executive jet came to a stop a hundred yards past the main terminal. The handsome young Arab was first out of his seat and stood by the main cabin door as it opened from the outside. He couldn't tell if he first felt the heat or heard the cheers from the thousands that waited for their first glimpse of "The Giver."

Mohamed walked back into the plane where Nathan stood giving last minute instructions to four gray suits. "You will stay on the plane until the crowd has left. I will see to your accommodation and send a car for you later," he said.

Thousands of voices cheered and screamed; it was almost deafening. They covered the airport runways from one end to the other; fifty thousand of them stood in the blistering heat, calling to him.

"Nathan, salaam, salaam, Nathan!"

Over and over, they shouted his name. As he reached the bottom of the gangway and placed his foot on sacred ground, the people of Arabia screamed with joy. A twenty-year-old boy from Vancouver, British Columbia, became the first Jew ever to be welcomed by a nation of Muslims.

"'The Giver' is here!" they screamed.

Two members of the royal family were first to greet him; both took his hand and kissed his cheek.

"Welcome, Giver. Welcome to our land. We have waited a long time."

There were at least twenty more waiting for an introduction. Nathan moved slowly down the line taking a moment to say something to each one of them. Some kissed his cheek; others shook and kissed his hand. All were not sincere, but now was not the time for persuasion.

An old man waited at the end of the line; his face was mostly covered but Nathan sensed he was someone important. He was strong and virile looking, but had a quizzical smile.

"Good morning, young sir," he said. The handshake was weak and tentative.

The old man leaned forward and whispered in Nathan's ear. "Should I be afraid? he said. "Shall I wonder if 'The Giver' is anything more than just a Jewish boy?"

Nathan stepped back and looked into his eyes and searched for the meaning in the old man's words. The two princes moved quickly and tried to hurry Nathan into the waiting limo.

"One moment, please, my friends," he said, as he placed his right hand on the old man's shoulder.

"Be not afraid, old man," he said. "I have a gift for you. Your heart doesn't see a Jewish boy, it sees 'The Giver,' with a gift of joy."

The old man covered his face and backed into the crowd.

Chapter Twenty-two

Deep beneath the surface, three men sat looking at the aerial photographs and classified documents that lay scattered on an oval table in front of them. Other top secret papers and FPEOs, *For the President's Eyes Only,* envelopes were on the floor. They had been seated in the dimly lit room for an hour. Their jackets hung on the back of their chairs as the world leaders pondered over what to do about 'The Giver.' The American president was the first to break the silence.

"What I don't understand is who kidnapped him in the first place? None of our sources have turned up anything to link it to any known terrorist group."

"It sounds like, what do you Americans say, 'an inside job.'" The Russian prided himself on his knowledge of American lore.

The Texan interjected, "I'm afraid, gentlemen, there is nothing in Nathan Roth's file to indicate he is anything other than what he and many others say he is: a young man with an idea, trying to fulfill a prophecy; and we can't kill an idea, can we?"

"We've been killing ideas from the beginning of time," said the Soviet chairman. "And as this 'Giver' has pointed out, nothing has changed."

"Well, we can't just allow him to control the world now, can we? We can't let a twenty-one-year-old kid dictate the way things are or will be. Let's be serious, gentlemen."

The oversized Asian took a long drag from his cigarette and blew a narrow stream of smoke into the overhead light.

"He is only twenty!" he said, as he tossed the dossier into the center of the table. "Accidents do happen; don't they, my friends?"

The American was quick to respond to the Chinese leader's remark.

"Accidents! This kid has an accident, and it will be far worse for all of us."

"What do you mean?" said the bald Russian.

"Disciples, man; the world would be thrown into chaos. There won't be one martyr, there'll be millions of them, tearing down bases and building day care facilities. It's too late for an accident; we need to make a decision and we need to make it now." The American's words tailed off to a mumble as he quickly read through the document just handed to him by an aid.

"I thought you said it was too late," said the man from Peking.

"That it was; that it was," said the president.

The Russian was growing annoyed with the unfocused president.

"What the hell are you reading?"

The American's eyes narrowed and focused on the document.

"We may have a solution to our problem, my friends. This was dispatched an hour ago; it seems our boys at the UN have given us the edge; if we can't kill him, maybe we can persuade him; we have his brother."

King Faisal determined oil production a job yes, but a job that would have serious world-wide consequences. It was not Nathan's intent to discuss such matters, but he was aware that the man who controlled the oil controlled not only Saudi Arabia, but also the men who until this day never shook the hand of a Jew.

They were seated cross-legged on small woven carpets against the walls of the great room in the palace of Riyadh. The young Mohamed stood behind Nathan and kept a watchful eye on the proceedings. King Faisal sat next to Nathan on a raised platform in the center of the room under a massive crystal chandelier

"Your Majesty," Nathan said, "do you believe life goes on after we die?" It was a whimsical question.

The king smiled and leaned next to him and whispered in his ear, "I don't know, Giver, but when I die, I will let you know."

Nathan had not expected the Saudi ruler to have a sense of humor. His sudden outburst of laughter caught everyone by surprise. As Nathan laughed so did the king, and as the king laughed so did the others. Soon everyone was laughing. Nathan tried to stop by falling, pushing his face into a soft silk cushion.

"You have a most infectious laugh," he said. "It's like the sun, warm and comforting; no wonder so many of our brothers love you."

"If it is only laughter I bring, Your Majesty, then my mission would be over."

"Tell me about the gift, Nathan?" the King of Saudi Arabia asked. "Is it OK that I call you Nathan?"

"Of course, Your Majesty, that is my name."

"Then you shall call me Abdul, for that is my name."

They spoke for hours; the king had many questions and Nathan was patient but not condescending.

"There are no limits to the gift of joy, my king," he said. "Once you have experienced it, once you realize it is a feeling, a feeling everlasting in the hearts of men who seek its power, a power beyond all others, a power that can change the world—you will see the truth in it.

"Why now, Nathan? What do you want from all this?"

"I have no agenda, my king. I have only come to deliver the gift. It will be up to you and the other great leaders to use the power of the gift."

Unexpectedly, the great king clapped his hands. "Come, my friend, you must be famished; we will eat. It will give me time to think about everything you have said."

Suddenly the youngest and the most precocious of the king's five daughters ran across the great room and fell into her father's lap.

"Father, Father!" she shouted. "Is this 'The Giver'?"

"Yes, my child, this is 'The Giver.'"

"I know who you are," she said, pointing her little finger and touching Nathan's hand, then quickly pulled it away.

"Don't be afraid, my child; he won't hurt you," said the king.

"But I might tickle you!"

Nathan's fingers walked up the little arm and tickled her neck. The little princess squealed and fell upon him. He held her like a doll, so precious and so fragile.

The king had already made a fateful decision. *A Jew has come with the gift of joy; who am I to argue with Allah's wisdom?*

The king watched them play in the pillows; his eyes disclosed the affection he suddenly felt for "The Giver."

After dinner, Nathan asked to be excused from further discussions. He was exhausted and needed sleep.

"Of course. You must rest before our journey."

"Our journey, my king?"

"Yes, tomorrow we will go to Ra's Al Khafji, my palace by the sea. You will love it there, Nathan, I promise."

Nathan didn't argue; he suspected the king had a good reason for the sudden change of plans. Mohamed was not of the same opinion.

"Not another plane trip, Master."

"Mohamed! How many times..."

"But maybe the king is not your friend. Maybe he plans to betray you, or lock us up so no one can find us."

"I need you there, Mohamed; you mustn't think you are only along for the ride. Soon your presence will be felt. Now go to sleep and try not to snore."

The handsome young Arab laid his head on the pillow and snored.

The following evening, Nathan and Abdallah stood on the highest balcony of the palace at Ra's Al Khafji. They could see for miles as the setting sun cast a million shades of orange across the Persian Gulf.

"Did I not tell you it was beautiful, Nathan?"

"You did, my king; but I am still puzzled why you brought me here."

"There are some, many in fact, who don't share your vision, Nathan. They are those who must be convinced of your power; you must win them over. I have sent invitations, they have yet to respond, but I am hopeful they will come."

"Why have you done this, Abdul? I did not ask..."

"I know you didn't, my friend; but I have decided to help you anyways. There is much you must learn before you meet the other Saudi leaders. If you can persuade my uncle, the warrior king, you will have persuaded your worst enemy. I cannot tell you how, Giver—only you know that. But since they consider me and my family the true leaders of Saudi Arabia, at least they will listen if I ask them to, and I have asked them to."

It was true; there was a lot to learn. Twelve hundred years of history and hatred for the infidels could not just simply be forgotten. It would take more than words to soften the hearts of the warriors. Killing Jews had become a way of life for them.

Days turned into a week and still no word from the fundamentalists. Nathan's growing concerns were discussed every day.

"Your hospitality is more than generous, my king," Nathan said, referring to the opulence of his personal quarters. "But, I must confess, I'm growing weary of waiting."

"Patience, my young friend; patience is the key to this undertaking. In the meantime, I have further proof of my undying friendship. I myself believe I am your greatest ally and truest friend—behold!" The king extended his arms and opened his palms motioning to the entrance beyond the marble pillars.

Layers of transparent white chiffon covered her from head to toe. A floor-length chain of orchids hung from her shoulders and trailed behind her. Petals fell to the floor as she moved towards him. Beams of light from the afternoon sun followed her and exposed the shape of her. Closer now, the light danced in her dark almond-shaped eyes. Her raven black hair fell over her narrow shoulders and a shear white veil covered her face. But now only a few feet away, he could never forget those eyes.

"Merriam," he whispered. He held her gently. She touched his face and kissed him on the cheek.

"Am I not the greatest friend in the world!" the king shouted.

That evening, their naked bodies glistened in the moonlight as they stood holding each other on the marble terrace overlooking the Sea of Many Colors.

"It's hard to believe it's the same moon we watched in Sudbury, isn't it, Nathan?"

"Yes, Merriam, I remember."

"Only there's no Cantor Nishi hiding in the bushes this time," she said.

He kissed her passionately on the mouth; he felt her soft breasts against his chest and felt her hands moving over him touching him everywhere. She broke from his embrace and ran across the white marble floor to the round white silk bed on the other side of the room.

"You can have me, if you can catch me!" she said, laughing.

A temptress, a woman so beautiful not even a prophet could resist. "Here I come."

They loved, laughed, and slept until late the following day.

Chapter Twenty-three

"This is Captain Aaron Roth, 077174, on orders from United Nations base Bahrain. My engines have failed and I'm going down; I am sending coordinates now."

Aaron repeated his mayday message three times before he jettisoned.

The narrow beam of light shining in his eyes made it impossible to see who was rescuing him.

"There he is!" Two men jumped into the sea and dragged him onboard the patrol boat.

"You are Captain Roth!" the dark-skinned commander insisted.

"I'm Captain Roth, thanks."

"Take him below and blindfold him; hurry!"

"But, hey, wait a minute, what's going on here?"

"Shut up, Jew!" he shouted. "Take him!"

"Come, come, my children!" King Faisal called out near the open entrance as Nathan and Merriam rested in each other's arms. "I have good news, Nathan! Come quickly!"

Nathan jumped from the bed and began dressing.

"You coming?"

"I think I'll just lie here for the rest of my life," she said.

"OK, I'll be right back; now don't go hiding on me again."

"What is it, Abdul? Tell me."

"They are coming, Nathan! All of them; it is better than I imagined."

"When, Abdul, when are they coming?"

"Three days from now; is that enough time, Nathan?"

"It will have to be; I'll call Sam, he'll inform the press."

"The press! I don't think the press will set the right mood. No, no, not the press…I'd have to tell them…they wouldn't come."

"Relax, my friend, they'll come. They wouldn't miss the chance to discredit me in front of the media. They'll come."

They came all right, from every sect and province, from every fundamentalist group and every anti-fundamentalist group. From all over Arabia they came. Some came in hopes that "The Giver" would heal ancient wounds and bring peace to the Middle East. Others came with hopes of exposing the Jew as a fraud.

Due to King Faisal's tutelage and insight, Nathan was now aware of several internal conflicts within the country. He had to be careful not to discuss them with those who might be offended.

The palace by the sea was considered a holy place; it gave some even more pause before agreeing to the presence of reporters, who now took their positions on either side of the great room. The one hundred and fifty guests sat at round linen covered tables. Nathan and King Faisal sat facing them on a raised platform behind a long table against the wall.

The king rose and moved to the dozens of microphones to make the introduction.

"Honored guests, it warms my heart to see old friends again. We come today not to talk but to listen. We shall not judge or be offended, for they are only words. The truth and beauty in these words have already brought me what was promised by him. He has already given his gift to me and to our people. I have heard the wisdom in the words and felt their power. Allow me to introduce Nathan, 'The Giver.'"

There was some applause, even a few cheers, but it wasn't the warmest of welcomes. Nathan moved to the microphones and began his address. Though his words were moving and passionate, there were still murmurs of distrust. He paused and looked at those with the most suspicious eyes, and spoke only to them.

"Young though I am, I have seen all there is to see in your heart. You cannot hide from the joy I bring. You cannot hide from the power of forgiveness. I am blind only to that which is hidden; I can see all that is truth. You are the fearless yet you hide from the light. You are the strongest of men yet your heart can be broken. I am but the bastard son of a tormented woman; if it's truth you seek then look no more.

"That which had remained locked in a stone box for two thousand years has been revealed. Will you cast it back and live that which history has lain upon you? Or do you live as it was intended, seeing all that is beautiful and joyous, as if it had never been taken from you? This is the gift I bring, a gift that, once given, will lead you into the light of understanding."

Many began to rise and called to him. "Nathan 'The Giver' is here!" From silence to mayhem and back again, their tears of joy gave many renewed strength of purpose. Arabs and Jews would soon stand together in peace and friendship.

"Your heart I sense is growing stronger; the gift of joy is everlasting; you can feel it now; it flows into you...you cannot stop it; it fills your heart and mind. Here it is, the gift of which I spoke."

Three remained seated, two young and one ancient warrior king. Their eyes revealed their lack of trust. Nathan moved to his left and stepped off the podium and walked towards the center of the room. He hadn't taken his eyes off the old man in the black robe and red sash. The infamous warrior king was also staring as Nathan stood and faced him.

"You have been taught something of our history, but I'm afraid it will take more than words from a Jewish boy to heal the past," he said.

"Don't be afraid, old man," Nathan said. "Your heart doesn't see a Jewish boy. It sees 'The Giver' with a gift of joy." Nathan grabbed the warrior king's shoulders and kissed him hard on both cheeks. Quickly, the warrior's sons jumped from their seats and appeared to brandish their knives.

"Hold your blades!" he said. The old warrior stood motionless and starred deeply into Nathan's eyes.

"Forgive me now, old man, and feel the power of the gift." The tension grew as the reporters moved to get a shot of the potential violence. A cool wind blew through the room as the late sun reflected off the gold leaf ceiling and onto the warrior king's softening expression.

"I will no longer be afraid," he said, and placed his hands on Nathan's shoulders and pulled him to his chest. The old warrior kissed him twice on both cheeks and embraced him like a father embraces a son.

"You are the light that was hidden from me," he said. "I feel the power of it."

The king wept on Nathan's shoulder as his sons touched and kissed Nathan's hands. Reporters' mouths hung open in disbelief; what started out to be Nathan's soon-to-be published failure had suddenly become a miracle. *MIRACLE! SAUDI WARRIORS FORGIVE!* Headlines appeared on front pages around the world.

Chapter Twenty-four

It was supposed to be a routine surveillance mission. Now Aaron was bound and blindfolded in the hold of an Egyptian patrol boat. He assumed it was Egyptian simply because that was of what he'd been taking pictures. Egypt had been amassing tanks and artillery on the Sinai Peninsula in what was, unquestionably, preparation for war with Israel. The United States and other countries were desperately trying to avoid another Arab-Israeli conflict. The United Nations had failed in their attempt to enforce the peace treaties and resolutions of 1949 and now the new Palestinian Liberation Organization as well as Syria had publicly decreed they would destroy Israel and take back what they had lost eighteen years earlier.

Aaron was sure he was still near the ocean; he had been pulled from the hold and tossed into the back of a truck; two hours later, still blindfolded, he was pulled from the truck as two men on either side guided him fifty yards up a few steps, down a hallway, and into a jail cell. He heard the sound of the heavy metal door being locked behind him.

"OK, Jew, you can take cloth off eyes."

Aaron removed the blindfold; his first look was of the overweight Arab who stood on the other side of the bars smiling at him. His uniform was a size too small and his teeth were ten different shades of yellow.

Under the miracle headlines, there were reports of the growing tensions in the Middle East. It was clear to Nathan that his success at Ra's Al Khafji would need to overshadow that tension and open new opportunities for peaceful dialogue between Israel and its Arab neighbors.

"I must caution you, Giver," the general said into the phone. "There are many who would not hesitate to use your death as a way to war."

"Thank you, General, I realize the risks. But I must tell you, I am not, nor will I let myself become involved in politics. I will be back in Jerusalem on the third; by then I will have met with every Arab leader in the region. The outcome of those meetings is not part of my mission. Goodbye, General."

Nathan hung up the phone and called to the handsome young Arab. "C'mon, Mohamed, it's time to leave for the airport."

"Yes, Master."

"Mohamed!"

"OK, Nathan, I'm ready."

Merriam wanted to go with him; she stood in front of him waiting for his embrace.

"I know you're not happy," he said, reaching for her. "But it's not safe enough, not yet. Soon it will be, and when it is, I will send for you."

She watched from the palace balcony as he entered the limo and drove off. She wondered if the King of Jordan would love him too.

Nathan waved to the crowds that lined the streets of Amman. The sun had set and thousands held candles and cheered as the ten-car procession came to a stop in front of the palace entrance. King Hussein descended the white marble steps and extended his hand to him. Nathan held the young king's hand with both of his.

"Salaam, Your Majesty. I am Nathan, the one they call 'The Giver.' I have come with a gift for you and for the people of Jordan."

"I and my people await you. Please, come; many have gathered; they must see you. I'm afraid none will leave until they do."

Nathan and the king stood between the white pillars of the highest balcony of the palace. Below in the courtyard and beyond the walls a hundred thousand candles glimmered in the darkness. A single microphone made it possible for all to hear "The Giver." He spoke in perfect Arabic.

"God, bless this place and all who gather here." From a muffled roar to high-pitched screams, the thousands below welcomed him. "I bring the gift of joy to the people of Jordan. Open your hearts to the power of the gift. Blessed are you who widen the path to forgiveness. I am 'The Giver.' Walk into the light and behold the truth of our humanity."

Nathan raised his arms outward and over the gathering.

"Oh mighty God, see how many have come to keep the promise of the gift. Let them feel what could not be felt; let them see what could not be seen; let them change what could not be changed. Oh loving God, let all who love You feel your gentle strength. Hold us tight and bind us forever to the power of the gift."

Nathan looked into the tearful eyes of the king. They were sad and pleading. Nathan reached out and drew him to his chest, kissing him gently on both cheeks. They turned and faced the cheering crowd. With their arms around each other, they waved once more to the people below.

It was off to Syria next, then Lebanon and the key visit to Egypt. Nathan was aware that Egypt, especially, was committed to the destruction of Israel. President Gamal Abdel Nasser had already sent civilian fighters into Israel, attacking small settlements and killing many Israeli civilians. That and his threat to close down and blockade the strait of Tiran would, if he did, bring immediate retaliation by Israel. If Nathan's visit to other Arab counties could prevent war, it would be his visit to Egypt that might start one.

President Charles Helou of Lebanon and President Nureddin al-Atassi of Syria tried to involve him in political discussion but Nathan graciously refused.

"I am not a politician," he said. "I care not what reasons men use to separate what is so common to us all. I seek only to bring the gift promised to you in the prophecy."

Neither of the Arab presidents was able to stop their people from welcoming "The Giver" any way they could. In Beirut he spoke from the steps of the Great Mosque. In Damascus he used a megaphone from the roof of his car. They gathered in groups of ten thousand and more. Through the streets of both capitals he stopped and spoke of the gift.

Chapter Twenty-five

Sam Weis sat on the bed in his hotel waiting for Nathan's call. He had thought of many ways to break the news to him; but no matter how he said it, Nathan's reaction was sure to be the same. The high-pitched shrill of the telephone sent shock waves through him.

"Hello, Sam, how are you? How's the prime minister?" Nathan's gentle voice was going to make it harder.

"The prime minister is well and ready for your meeting. I'm fine, but I…I…"

"What is it, Sam? What's happened?"

"It's your brother, Nathan; he's been shot down and taken prisoner by the Egyptians."

There was a long silence before Nathan spoke again.

"Are you sure it's the Egyptians, Sam? It's very important that you are sure."

"Well, it didn't come from a government official, but we know he was picked up near the Egyptian base at Al Ghardaqua, on the Red Sea."

"How do you know this, Sam?"

"Israeli intelligence intercepted it as well as picking up your brother's distress signal before he bailed out. The message came from someone calling his family telling them he was guarding 'The Givers' brother. It originated from Al Ghardaqua."

"But, to your knowledge, Sam, does President Nasser know anything about it?"

"I have no knowledge of that, Nathan."

"OK, Sam, please say nothing more to anyone about this until you hear from me. I'm flying out of Damascus in an hour."

"But, Nathan, what will we do about your brother?"

"My brother is a very resourceful person. Don't speak of this again, Sam, is that clear?"

"Yes, I guess it is. Goodbye, Nathan."

"Goodbye, Sam."

The handsome young Arab watched as his beloved friend placed the phone back on its cradle and covered his face with both hands.

"What is it, Master? What can I do?" Nathan slowly removed his hands from his face and looked at him.

"I think it is time to make your presence felt, my young friend."

Nathan hadn't thought about those who chased him on the California highway or even the man who held the top of the Jack Daniel's bottle since he arrived in Israel. Suddenly he knew what he must do; if they could get to his brother, it was clear they could get to the rest of his family.

In Los Angeles, California, Val Belkin sat at the bar that wrapped around one side of the cabana at the far end of the pool. Mary was fixing him a drink while he absorbed the headlines of the *Los Angeles Times*.

"I wish we could get the press your illustrious son gets," he said, smiling.

"I wonder who his agent is, Val."

"By all accounts, my love, his agent is not of this world."

They both laughed; it had become a constant occurrence. After almost thirty years of torment, Mary was finally happy. Val was attentive and kind and loved her more than he had loved anyone. Mary continued to write and Val continued to direct and produce her music. The phone on the bar rang.

"Hello," Mary answered.

"Is this Missus Mary Roth, please?" The voice had a polite Italian accent.

"Yes, this is Mary Roth, who's this?"

"Missus Roth, my name is Tony D'Angelo; I am a very good friend of Nathan's, 'The Giver.' I am here in Los Angeles and I would like to come to see you. I have a message from your son. Will three o'clock be convenient?"

Mary agreed and the three of them sat around a glass table on the patio a few hours later.

"Your son has touched the hearts of millions, Missus Roth. I feel very fortunate to have known him personally."

Don D'Angelo talked about Nathan in a way Mary had never heard before. He told her how he and many from Little Europe knew and loved him and how they would do anything to help and protect him, including his family.

"Please, Missus Roth and Mister Val, there are some who would try to hurt Nathan through his family. I want you to keep these two men here with you." Tony pointed to the two heavy-set gentlemen in black suits who stood at the far end of the pool.

"They will stay in your house until Nathan tells you himself that it is all right for them to leave. It is very important to your son that you do this; for your protection, you understand. They will be with you wherever you go, twenty-four hours a day. They are professional men and do not require more than one bed to sleep in. Please, Missus Roth?"

It took a few moments, but after some details were worked out, Mary and Val agreed to everything. Tony wasn't optimistic he would be as successful as in Seattle.

Lovey dropped the newspaper into the open garbage bin at the back of the Pike Street service station

"Piss on the little prick. I don't care who he calls himself; he's still the guy that wasted Bruno and Mickey. He's going to pay, one way or the other. His father and sister live in Vancouver so we're going to pay them a little visit, aren't we, Tootie?" The miniature poodle wiggled and barked in her arms. A tall black man finished filling the tank of the black Cadillac as two others stamped out their cigarettes on the pavement behind her.

"Let's go, boys! It's a three-hour drive. I want to be there before dark."

Lovey's driver turned the ignition and honked at the white van that had backed up in front of them. A heavy-set man in overalls got out of the driver's seat and placed the nozzle of the gas pump into the open cap at the back of the van. The second honk was completely ignored.

"Back up then, for crying out loud!" Lovey grumbled from the back seat. As her driver turned to back up another white van moved in behind them.

Tony D'Angelo slid into the seat next to Lovey in the back of the Cadillac.

"What the hell. Who are..."

Tony D'Angelo didn't need any introduction. One look and Lovey knew exactly who sat next to her.

"You're a long way from Toronto, aren't you, Lovey? One might think you have forgotten about us."

"Don D'Angelo! I would never forget you," she said.

"Maybe you forgot where you came from and who finances you. Maybe you forgot your promises?" Lovey had missed several loan payments; it was this she was sure that had brought the godfather to Seattle.

"Business has been bad ever since that Jew boy killed Bruno," she said. "I'm going to even the score tonight."

Tony jerked Lovey's skirt up over her waist and grabbed the Beretta from her thigh and held the barrel to her ribs.

"You're not going anywhere, especially Vancouver. You got Bruno killed by sending him after Nathan. You got a Mickey killed by sending him after Nathan."

"But, Don D'Angelo, how do you know about that…"

Tony slapped her hard across her face. "You will never speak about Nathan again! He is my personal…" Don D'Angelo stopped himself. "I cannot trust you—this was a waste of time." Tony got out of the Cadillac and walked over to a black limo that had pulled into the station a moment earlier. Pausing for a few seconds, he gave instructions to the men in the van.

"Give the drivers an option. Get rid of her."

Manny leaned on the wrought iron fence overlooking Vancouver's inner harbor. The Lions Gate Bridge that connected the city to West Vancouver was a hundred feet below him. He could see for miles across the Straits of Georgia to the island and east up the Indian Arm. Summer in Vancouver…no question that when it wasn't raining it was the most beautiful city in the world. It was still early; the usual throng that spent their Sundays in Stanley Park hadn't arrived. Only a few lonely people like Manny and the dark stranger standing only a few feet away got up this early, unless they were going to church.

"What a beautiful city you have here; only my beloved Palermo is equal," he said. "My name is Tony." Manny thought it a little intrusive but accepted the stranger's handshake.

"Manny, Manny Roth," he said. "You're Italian?"

"Yes, but I've been living in Toronto for many years; this is my first trip to Vancouver."

"Ah, I'm in Toronto several times a year on business myself. What brings you to our fair city, Tony?"

Nathan hadn't seen Manny in almost five years; he could only tell Tony that his father was a difficult man and was probably upset and lonely since his mother left.

"He likely will resent being watched, Don D'Angelo," Nathan warned.

"Don't worry, Nathan. I'll a take care of everything," he said.

"Oh, business…uh, excuse me. I hope you don't a mind, but did you say your name was Roth?" Tony asked.

"Yes, Roth. Why?"

"This is a miracle!" Manny could see the excitement on the stranger's face. "You are Emmanuel Roth; you are 'The Givers' father. This is more than a miracle!"

Manny read the papers every day, but other than with Lizzy, he hadn't discussed his son with anyone. In fact, he wasn't even sure it was anything more than a hoax. Moreover, he hadn't talked to his son since Bubba died, and didn't know if he ever would again.

"I'm afraid my son has long forgotten me. I can't really blame him. I haven't been the best of fathers, and well…I guess I haven't been the best of anything for some time now."

"Now a you look here, Mister Roth. Your son, he loves you. This I know."

"That's kind of you to say, but not true."

Tony placed his hand on Manny's shoulder. "Mister Roth, I have not been honest with you."

Manny raised his head and looked at Tony through tear-filled eyes. "Honest with me? I don't understand."

"You will understand this. I am friend and follower of 'The Giver.' He has sent me to watch over his family and protect you from those who would try to stop him from bringing peace to the world. Come, my friend. I will tell you everything about your wonderful son."

Tony told Manny of his friendship with his son and how Nathan had become loved by so many in Little Europe. He told him of the millions who believed in him and the power of the gift.

"I have taken your son into my heart," he said. "He is my life, my family. There is nothing I would not do to help and protect him and his father."

Manny's two bodyguards stood on either side of him as they watched Tony's plane take off from the Vancouver airport. There had never been a time in his life he had felt this much pride either in himself or anyone else.

"'The Giver' asks for your forgiveness," Tony told him. "He is sorry for not being there for you; but soon the whole world will know the power of the gift, and when that day comes you will be standing next to him, exactly where you belong."

Manny folded the evening paper under his arm and looked at his two companions. "Let's go, gentlemen. How about a steak? I'm starving."

It was June 2, 1967.

Chapter Twenty-six

Sam had received dozens of calls from Israeli cabinet ministers, pleading with him to cancel Nathan's visit to Cairo. They all had different ways of putting it, from it's not safe to they'll kill him on site. Nasser had blockaded Israel's only access to the Suez and had built up defense positions all across the Sinai. Prime Minister Eshkol himself had tried to contact him but Nathan was unavailable, so he told Sam, "Now is not the time."

Sam replied, "Tell the prime minister I am not a politician, but I will do all I can."

From the airport to the presidential palace they stood ten deep. Nathan held the crossbar and stood tall in the open-air limo as it slowly made its way through the streets of Cairo. He waived sometimes with both hands over his head, blessing them as he passed by. They numbered in the hundreds of thousands, screaming and hollering the high-pitched shrill of celebration.

President Nasser held out his hand and assisted Nathan from the limo in front of the palace. He was dressed in a light blue suit with a white tie. He was much taller than Nathan and as handsome as anyone he had ever seen.

"Welcome, salaam, Nathan."

"Salaam, Mister President. Thank you for inviting me." They had to shout to be heard. The two men walked up the steps together and stopped on the last of twenty, turned and faced the adoring people standing in the great square. Nathan waved one more time before entering through the massive double doors.

Inside the sound of cheers was replaced with the sound of clicking cameras.

"This way, Mister President, please. This way, Giver, now together please, thank you."

President Nasser gave a slight nod to an assistant.

"That will be all for now, everyone. There will be an opportunity for photos later this afternoon. Thank you; thank you."

"Perhaps we might sit awhile, Mister President," Nathan suggested. "I've been standing since leaving the airport."

"Of course; this way, Nathan."

He was lead into a large room off the foyer. Nathan and the president sat in large high-backed chairs against the far wall; a small oval coffee table separated them as they sat at a slight angle facing each other.

"Excuse me, Mister President. This man says he is with him," said the uniformed man standing in the doorway holding Mohamed's arm.

"Yes, he is. Please allow him to come and refresh himself," Nathan said.

Nasser reacted quickly. "No! He can wait outside."

"Mister President, this is my interpreter, and close friend. My Arabic is...well, let's say not as good as I would like it, you understand?"

"All right," he said, and motioned to Mohamed to stand behind Nathan and to the side.

There was a sudden coldness to the president's demeanor; the cheerful and welcoming face was no longer smiling at his young guest.

"I will not be intimidated by your government," he said. "I am not a fool, even though my people think you a God."

Nathan remained silent for the moment. Nasser turned and glared at the handsome Mohamed.

"How is it you, an Arab, work for a Jew?" he said.

"I do not work for him. I am friend and follower of 'The Giver.'"

"But, he's still a Jew; aren't you, Nathan Roth?" Nasser's hardening expression made it clear he wasn't a believer.

Nathan took a small sip from the glass of water he took from the oval coffee table.

"We can never have enough friends, wouldn't you agree, Mister President?" Nathan waited for Nasser to answer.

"Hmm, yes...I see."

"I have come as a man in need of friends, Mister President. My heart and mind are one in this." Nasser appeared puzzled at Nathan's words. "Some men can only think; other men can only feel. It is when both are as one that men are truly free." Nasser remained silent and confused. "I have come with a gift for you, Mister President. It does not come from an Israeli or a Jew, or an Arab or a Christian. It is a gift of humanity—which is common to all who love God. Give us our humanity and see that which cannot be seen, feel that which cannot be felt, change that which cannot be changed. Those living in the past or the future—places that do not exist—live without humanity." Nasser was thinking now.

"It matters not what others believe; let them be free to believe whatever they wish. The power of our humanity is greater than anyone's belief." Nasser was now staring at "The Giver."

"All that is fear, hatred and despair live in our thoughts, in places that do not exist. Walk into the light where everything that is beautiful can be seen touched or changed. It is the power of the gift." Nathan looked deeply into Nasser's eyes. "It will set you free, Abdel. It will fill your heart with joy. Feel the joy, Abdel; feel it now as it was intended."

Nathan stood and reached out to the man whose arms felt too light, whose eyes were too watery and whose anger had disappeared.

"I am the light, 'The Giver.' Come, Abdel. Forgive me now and feel the joy in your heart." Abdel Nasser rose from his chair and embraced "The Giver," kissing him over and over again on his cheeks.

"I have heard the wisdom of your words. I was wrong to doubt you. I tried to ignore the gift; I was afraid. I am no longer afraid. Please tell the people of Israel I am recalling my army from the Sinai. There will be no war between us."

It was June 3, 1967.

Chapter Twenty-seven

Photos of Nathan waving to the thousands in Cairo covered the front pages once again, except for the small caption at the bottom: *U.S. Troops Number 500,000 in Vietnam.*

Cantor Nishi laid the paper on the bed next to him. Of all people, he who discovered "The Giver" had hardly been consulted about anything. Sam was always too busy organizing Nathan's itinerary to speak to him. He had been virtually discarded by Nathan; no one asked him for advice, spiritual or otherwise. His frustration and anger had reached their limit when he was almost denied a seat in the Knesset for Nathan's address to the world.

Moesha Tosker sat at the head of the long mahogany table. Ten uniformed officers on either side continued to look over the array of aerial surveillance photos as the general was handed a message. He excused himself and picked up the phone from the desk in the adjoining room.

"This is General Tosker, go ahead."

"General, this is Nathan."

"Nathan! Where are you?"

"I'm in the air; we've just left Cairo. General, I have an important message for you."

"Yes, Nathan, go on."

"General, I have been assured by President Nasser that he intends to withdraw his forces from the Sinai. Did you get that?" There was suddenly a lot of crackling noises on the line.

"I'm sorry, Nathan, could you repeat that?"

"The Egyptians are withdrawing from the Sinai."

"I'm sorry, Nathan, you're breaking up. Perhaps you should try a different frequency."

Nathan repeated the message three more times, but still the general was unable to acknowledge it.

"We will be in Jerusalem in two hours, I will talk to you then," Nathan said, handing the headset back to the co-pilot.

General Tosker put his index finger on the phone button then released it.

"This is General Tosker, get me Granville at UNAFB Bahrain and ask Cantor Nishi to come to my office.

Aaron scratched another line on the stone wall beside his cot as the oversized Arab opened his cell. He called him Old Yeller Teeth.

"Come, Jew!" he said. "It's time to call your brother." Holding his automatic rifle in one hand, Old Yeller Teeth tossed a set of handcuffs at Aaron. "Put on, Jew pig," he demanded.

Aaron hadn't seen the light of day in a month. The small window near the ceiling of his cell was the only way he knew night from day. Now, as he was pushed out the door of the small building and across the compound, he could see six or seven other buildings. It was obviously a military base of some kind; two barracks on the left, a couple of ordnance buildings on the right. There was a water tower at the far end and a wire fence, which was in need of major repairs, surrounded the entire post. Old Yeller Teeth pushed him to the left around a small shack where fifty feet in front of him a man in an Egyptian uniform raised an Egyptian flag on a newly painted pole. Old Yeller Teeth used the barrel of his rifle to direct Nathan to his left, up three stairs to one of the larger wood sided buildings, and down a narrow hall to a small room where two uniformed Egyptians sat on wooden stools behind a small metal table. A black telephone was wired to the back wall and placed in front of him. Old Yeller Teeth removed the handcuffs and pushed Aaron into the armchair facing the two officers.

"Captain Roth, I hope your stay with us has been a pleasant experience," said the Egyptian. "Soon you will be reunited with your brother and this will all be over." The dark-skinned officer was the same man who had pulled Aaron from the Red Sea and threw him in the hold of the patrol boat.

"You're going to make a call to your brother," he said. "You will tell him that we will kill you unless he does exactly what it says in the package he has been given. You will say nothing else or it will be the last thing you ever say. Is that clear?"

Jews from all over the world had come home to the Promised Land. Dark ones from Africa, light ones from Europe, all had come to escape prejudice and oppression. They came with a renewed spirit and purpose. Never again would they allow another nation to torture and murder them like animals. If their Arab neighbors wanted to destroy them, then so be it. Only this time they could fight back, but not from hidden tunnels in the sewers of Warsaw and not with bottles of gasoline thrown at passing Nazi tanks. This was different; they now had an army of Jews, chosen by God to keep what was taken from them twelve hundred years ago.

Sam Weis's 707 taxied up to and stopped in front of the main terminal at Ben Gurion International. As Nathan stood on the gangway at the top of the stairs he heard no cheering. There weren't the thousands that had greeted him in Cairo or Amman or even Baghdad. There were at least two hundred reporters and photographers and a number of government officials on the tarmac, but there were no citizens of Israel. For a week now Israeli newspapers had run editorials calling Nathan a friend of the Arabs and not of Israel. They called him a turncoat and a traitor. They said he'd been brainwashed by tyranny and had been living off the wealth of Arab kings and dictators. The government of Israel had made it clear; those who greeted "The Giver" at the airport would be themselves traitors. What the government had not foreseen were the thousands who would decide to ignore the order and now lined the streets of Jerusalem, cheering.

Military police had been diverting traffic away from the airport since early in the morning. It didn't take long for the people of Jerusalem to figure out what was happening.

Sam looked at Nathan as they drove through Jerusalem in Sam's white limo.

"I guess their plan has backfired," he said.

"I guess so, Sam. What time am I to speak tomorrow?"

"Ten o'clock; you're the hottest ticket in town."

"I see, and who is waiting to see me?"

"Well, let's see. First there's the prime minister, then General Tosker, followed by Cantor Nishi—he's really pissed off. And last, but not least, is you know who."

"You mean Merriam, of course?"

"Yes, Giver, she's scared of what the papers said and she fears for your safety."

"I understand, Sam, but I cannot see her now. Please tell her I'm sorry. I assume everything is on schedule with our friends."

"It is, Nathan. They should be somewhere off the Egyptian coast by now."

The long awaited meeting between Nathan and the Israeli prime minister was at hand. Nathan believed this would be the defining moment, a moment where the Israeli commander-in–chief, a very religious man but completely convinced of Israel's ability to defend and destroy and control the entire Arab world, would be given 'the Gift.'

Nathan's understanding of what he had to do and why those who would oppose him would eventually expose themselves and make it clear to the prime minister that the road to joy and happiness and peace and freedom for the people of Israel could only be accomplished by accepting and believing in the prophecy. Nathan's own beliefs were going to be tested for the first time. From the moment he woke from the coma until now it had been a journey; he hadn't stopped to question its outcome, but now he felt the pangs of apprehension and doubt. What if the prophecy was just an ancient piece of paper or the ranting's of a mad man? What if it didn't matter how clear things were to him and maybe to millions of others? If the prime minister didn't accept the gift, it could all come crashing down.

Prime Minister Eshkol had waited patiently but as the double doors to the presidential suite opened Nathan's heart filled with anticipation.

"Good afternoon, Mister Prime Minister, I am Nathan Roth. Shalom."

"Shalom, Nathan. Please come in. This is your suite. I hope you'll be comfortable. Is there anything you would like, coffee perhaps?"

"No, nothing. Thank you. Mister Prime Minister, we have urgent matters to discuss. Please excuse your people so we may talk in private."

The prime minister was taken aback, but agreed to Nathan's request and dismissed a number of aids to another room.

"I have wonderful news, Prime Minister. I bring a personal message from President Nasser; he is pulling back from the Sinai. Your northern neighbors, the Syrians, are also halting military action. I have other messages from Jordon and Lebanon as well, and His Majesty the King of Saudi Arabia extends a personal invitation to his country. It is time, Mister Prime Minister. Will you welcome your neighbors and accept the gift of forgiveness?"

"You are mistaken," Prime Minister Eshkol insisted. "My generals have told me only moments ago that they are marching on us as we speak. It is too late for forgiveness; our forces are ready to retaliate."

"Would one of those generals be General Tosker?"

"Yes! Why?"

"I told General Tosker four hours ago of the Egyptian withdrawal."

"You have no proof of this! I can't believe my most trusted commander would lie to me."

"I don't care what you believe, Prime Minister. But if you're going to believe anything, you better believe what I'm telling you now. I have a gift for the people of Israel; if you stop me from delivering that gift you will be responsible for perpetuating hatred towards them. You, sir, are a politician; you would do anything to protect your way of thinking. I care not what you think! I care only that you trust in the power I have just given you and the fact that all military aid to Israel, provided by Mister Weis, will be cut off unless you withdraw the strike order at once!"

"I protest! This is outrageous! You will leave our people without protection; we will be crushed and thrown back into the sea."

"You have been deceived, Prime Minister. I will prove it to you when General Tosker and Cantor Nishi arrive. Please take a seat in the other room. I have arranged for you to hear our conversation. Afterwards, you have my permission to be as outraged as you like. Now, I believe the people of Israel are calling. Won't you join me?"

Nathan stood on the small balcony overlooking the street that fronted the King David Hotel. Thousands of Israelis had waited all day for this moment. Nathan was dressed in a white shirt and jeans, and he raised his arms over the people and shouted, "Shalom, Chavareem!"

In the street below, General Tosker covered his ears as he and Cantor Nishi passed through the crowd and entered the hotel lobby.

"They're here, Nathan." Sam led the prime minister to the adjoining room before opening the door to the suite.

"Good evening, General."

"Good to see you, Giver.

"Ah, and, Rabbi, hello, how are you?"

"I'm fine, Nathan, just fine."

"Please, gentlemen, sit; can I get you something, a drink perhaps?"

"No, nothing." Cantor Nishi quickly moved to the sofa and took out a handkerchief and wiped his forehead.

"You, General?"

"No, I'm fine, Giver." General Tosker took a seat in the chair to the left of the sofa and carefully placed a large brown manila envelope on the coffee table in front of him.

"I see Prime Minister Eshkol was unable to join us," said the general.

No one answered as Sam took a seat at the opposite end of the room near the balcony and watched as Nathan began pouring himself a glass of water from the pitcher on the table behind the sofa.

"Well, gentlemen, I imagine there must be something important you wish to talk about."

A thousand miles away, the handsome young Arab was first to jump from the helicopter into the murky waters of the Red Sea. The chopper stayed thirty feet above as Doran and ten others climbed into the two inflatable rafts. Timing was everything; the chopper could stay in the air only forty minutes. If it was going to have enough fuel to return to the helipad on Sam Weis's converted luxury yacht, everything had go perfectly.

Into the darkness the fearless eleven paddled their way to the rocky beach at Al Ghardaqua.

"Yes, Nathan," said Cantor Nishi. "It's about your speech tomorrow; we...that is, the general and I wish you to make certain statements regarding the current military actions of our enemies. This envelope contains those statements."

"General, I know you received my message about the Egyptian withdrawal; why would there be need for further comment?"

"There are other things to consider!" said the cantor.

"I can't imagine what that would have to do with me. I have told everyone in the Middle East that I have not nor will I participate in any political agendas."

"Nathan," the general's voice was less offensive, "perhaps if you read the statements first, then made up your mind."

"There is no need, General. I know what they say."

"But you couldn't! You..." Nishi was angry, angry with Nathan and angry at the notion that Israelis might not have the opportunity to rid themselves of the Arab threat.

Nathan cut the cantor off in Hebrew. "You have betrayed my trust!" he said. "You have come to terrorize and shame me. I will not play a part in your ruthless game."

Again the general showed his calmness. "Giver, there are many who worship and adore you; for their sakes, maybe it would be better if…"

"Quiet!" Nathan confronted the general. "You, and the other enemies of peace, have lost what I have given you. You have thrown away your humanity for political gain; I will have no part of it, or you. You are excused…leave me."

"You! You, child!" screamed the cantor. "What do you know of the enemies of Israel? You have spent months flying around in your jet, with no understanding of those who want to destroy us. They stand at our borders, waiting to slaughter us." The cantor had lost all composure.

Nathan looked deeply into the old man's eyes.

"It was you, Cantor, you had me kidnapped. You were the only one who knew my arrival time, and it was you who killed David Chechik; you and your terrorist friends. I don't know what kind of deal you made with them or what you thought you might gain from it. It was you who betrayed me and all who have chosen peace and freedom. You are my Judas."

General Tosker looked at his watch.

"Perhaps there is another way to convince you." The phone next to Sam rang out. "It's for you, Nathan," Sam said. "It's Aaron."

Eleven fearless and brave Palestinians had moved forward taking up positions behind the rocks. Doran and five others waited while his son and four others crawled up and over the sandy bank of the south beach. Mohamed could see the dark outline of the wooden buildings. He was only a hundred feet from the wire fence; two clicks of his flashlight signaled the others forward. Now together, Doran and his men moved toward the fence. Oddly, there was no need for the wire cutters; most of the fence had fallen and left easy access to the compound. There were several small buildings but only two could be seen with light coming from their windows.

"We will take the small one; you, the other. If he is in yours, you know what to do. If not? Return to the boat as fast as you can."

"Yes, Father, I understand."

Nathan took the phone from Sam and spoke to his brother.

"Aaron, don't say anything As soon as the door opens in front of you, hit the floor. If you understand, say hello Nathan and then say what they want."

"Hello, Nathan."

General Tosker, hearing Nathan's instructions, moved quickly to the door.

"Going somewhere, General?" Two gray suits and two Israeli officers stopped the general from making a quick exit. General Tosker turned and faced "The Giver."

"This was not my idea, 'Giver.' Please believe me."

"I do believe you, General," he said. "Please tell these officers who else was responsible and just possibly your soul will be saved. Do you concur, Mister Prime Minister?"

"Indeed I do, 'Giver.' Indeed I do!"

Mohamed kicked in the door and fired at the two by the table, sending them backward and killing them instantly.

Old Yeller Teeth dropped his weapon and fell to his knees screaming, "No, no, please. I am civilian. I am friend!"

"No! Don't kill him; he's not worth it," Aaron said.

"Captain Roth, hurry! We must go...now!"

Aaron grabbed Old Yeller Teeth's rifle lying next to him and jumped to his feet.

"OK, let's get the hell out of here."

Chapter Twenty-eight

The newly constructed Knesset glistened in the morning light. Thousands of people, many who slept overnight on stone streets, surrounded the white building waiting to catch a glimpse of "The Giver." Loudspeakers had been installed outside on the tops of government vehicles and lampposts. Television and radio equipment were everywhere. This would be the first time that television transmissions would bounce off orbiting satellites so people all over the world would hear and see Nathan speak live from Israel. Inside the great hall people were taking there designated seats. The Knesset's main chamber was designed to hold three hundred, but desks had been removed so that over seven hundred, including interpreters, could be seated. Television cameras were set up in every corner with one on wheels that roamed in front of the podium.

The first to enter were, of course, Israel's thirteen cabinet ministers who now took their seats in the front row. Behind them were rows of dignitaries from every nation, some still standing and shaking hands with their counterparts. Sam and Merriam sat next to King Faisal; his arch rival, the warrior king, his hand resting on the king's shoulder, whispered something in his ear. Presidents of Lebanon and Syria stood and welcomed each other with open arms and kisses. Cheers from the galleries exploded as Prime Minister Eshkol and President Nasser, walking hand in hand, entered the hall from behind the podium.

From every nation in the Middle East they came; religious leaders of every faith, of every culture and of every color. They came not as kings and dictators but as followers of "The Giver." Each and every person in the assembly came to be near him and share the power of the gift.

The double doors at the back of the Knesset opened. Photographers clicked and flash bulbs exploded as Nathan walked through the entrance. His tailored suit was the color of desert sand. His white cotton shirt and Israeli blue tie gave the perfect contrast to his dark tan and sandy blond hair. The cheers grew louder as Nathan descended the stairs leading to the podium. This was his dream: to bring joy and happiness to all humanity; to share with the entire world the power of the gift.

There was no let up as the crowd continued to applaud. The applause raised to another level as Nathan walked up the five stairs and stood behind the mahogany railing.

Raising his right hand, silence fell over the assembly.

"Good morning, my name is Nathan Roth."

"Mama, Mama! Come quick; it's starting!

"Oh look! There he is. Look! Look, it's Nathan!"

Papa Sharnofsky and Tony D'Angelo had no choice but to make room as Mama Sharnofsky sat down next to them in front of the TV.

"Oh look, Papa, doesn't he look wonderful?"

"Shush, Mama, he wants us to listen."

Lizzy, Manny and his two grandchildren sat around the living room in Vancouver.

"God, Dad, he looks like a movie star."

"More than a movie star, I think."

Michael, Ginny and wide-eyed little Taylor screamed with delight.

"Daddy, Daddy! Look! It's Uncle Nathan."

"I know, I know."

Mary tapped her champagne glass with a silver spoon and announced to her guests, "OK, everyone! Ladies and gentlemen, I give you my son Nathan, 'The Giver.'"

Nathan began in Hebrew. "The journey begins today. Men and women from every nation, from every religion, from every corner of our world, have chosen to tear down a mighty barrier, a barrier so high and so wide that for two thousand years it kept us from seeing the light. There are still some who hide from the light; I will visit them soon."

The tall Texan, the overweight Asian, and the bald Russian squirmed in front of their TV sets.

"There is no sword sharp enough to cut the bonds that bind us to the power of the gift. There is no bomb big enough to destroy that which cannot be seen by those who have never felt the power of the gift." Nathan spoke in Arabic.

"The hour glass has been turned on its side. What was and what might be no longer exist; our journey cannot take us there. The power of the light is ever lasting; it cannot be measured in time; it can only be seen or felt in the absence of time."

Nathan found the eyes of the warrior king. "Who could imagine a Jewish boy and an Arab king? Worlds apart, and yet, in an instant, found kindness, love and forgiveness in one embrace?" Nathan looked at Abdel Nasser. "Who could imagine that in an instant, a thousand years of hatred and fear would end simply because two men walked into the light and found the strength they needed to forgive that which no longer exists? I am 'The Giver,' and I have a gift for you."

Nathan raised his right hand and opened his palm upward. "It is unwrapped and uncolored. It is transparent yet it sparkles. It is heavy yet I can hold it high above my head without effort. It has no name yet it was born to me. I can hold it in my hand." Nathan closed his fist. "Yet it is more powerful than me." He looked into the TV camera just below him to the left and spoke in English. "I have a gift for you. It shall comfort you all the days of your life. It is cool yet warm. It is firm yet soft. It is weightless yet it fills your heart. It is still yet it moves through the universe to brighten every star. Look into the eyes of the person next to you and behold the power of the gift."

People outside the Knesset and millions around the world did just that. Their eyes filled with tears and the feeling of joy entered their hearts and minds.

From the top of the stairs on the left, three men entered the Knesset and walked down towards the podium. Nathan held his hand above his eyes to block out the camera light as the handsome young Arab, his father and Aaron stood with their backs to the wall. Their smiles and glowing faces brought tears to 'The Giver's' eyes. Nathan raised both arms over the gathering, bowed his head and prayed.

"Oh loving God, bless this place and all who gather here. Blessed are we who feel the power of the gift. Blessed are the children who love You so. Blessed is the light of understanding so clear and bright. Blessed is he who walks the path of forgiveness so others may know the power of the gift. Oh mighty God, cast out all that is hidden. Untie the bonds of time and let loose the power of the gift. Unravel the mystery of that which cannot be seen or felt."

Nathan lifted his head but kept his arms up and out over the gathering.

"Come into the light and feel what God intended. Come with me into the light; let it cover you and hold you strong and steadfast. I have a gift for you; come to me and feel its power. Come Christian, I see you. Walk to me now; walk, as Jesus walked into the light." A few people rose and began to walk toward the podium. "Come, Jew, I can see you. Walk to me; walk into the light as Moses did. Come, Muslim, there is plenty to see. Come to me, and walk into the light, as Mohamed walked toward the power of the light."

The handsome young Arab was first in line, followed by a stately old woman who looked into the eyes of her father's grandson and kissed his hand. Dina Kimberly Smyth's search for her father ended that day in Jerusalem.

THE END

Epilogue

One after another they came and kissed his hand; princes and kings; men of wealth, power and position. Was this the beginning of peace and joy? Could forgiveness be exchanged for hatred and fear? Was the prophesy fulfilled? Was Nathan's gift so simple? These are the questions that those people who depend on their ability to convince us to focus on past and future events, dictate and determine how we act in the present.

For thousands of years, priests have told us that love will save the world. Just love, everybody. But it's difficult to love someone who's shooting at you. Once again countries are invaded and occupied. And once again governments tell us that it will be better for everyone down the road. The problem is, we get "down the road" and nothing has changed; in fact, it's worse.

Nothing good can come from violence. No one feels good killing anything. Understand that everything that joins us together, everything that is beautiful in the human being, is simply the power to give joy to another. In return you get to feel exactly how God had intended you to feel...good! This is our power, the power to feel good when we do something good. The emphasis is on the doing, the action. When we do good, we feel good. It is a powerful automatic response; we can't stop it.

The power of the gift lies in man's acceptance of his humanity and his belief that all that is beautiful and good exists only in the present. We give up our power when we allow the thoughts of the past and our expectations of the future to lure us away from using our power. Hopelessness, hatred, fear, frustration, despair and depression live and fester in our thoughts of the past and the future. Kindness, happiness, love and joy live in our power to feel good simply by doing something good. Nathan believed in the clear simplicity of man's power to change. He imagined millions of people going around doing good things to each other every day and feeling good about it at the same time. Imagine what the world would be like if there was suddenly *A Change of Presence*? Nathan felt the power of the gift when he forgave his father. He believed that the world would also change. I hope all of us do.

Who would come from periled sea, with foreign tongue a rogue is he; a man so strange but not afraid, a home he built with hands and spade
The girl he found would give to him a son so small, so short and thin. The years gave way to sudden fame but no one knew from where it came

I give to you a sister, small, as sweet and dear as timbers tall. But it wasn't she who turned his heart; a son would come to tear apart
A son afraid they knew not why, he left no tears but others cried. Like ancient myths he did not bring, a son to him was the sting

Take your hand and place it here she spoke so low only he could hear. The night laid cover to their love with candles bright from above
Whispers heard from where they lay meant someone close was on his way. What claim is this you spew, he said, if truth it is then I am dead

She held him closer less he flees, who's to say it isn't thee. Her father's wishes did offend, from worlds apart she told him then; what time there was would come to pass, it mattered not their love would last. What future task it wasn't clear their love was now and not of fear

A boy so fair and wise was he that nations bent so all could see; a planet torn from within would not stand if made of sin.
From far and wide they said of him, this man's a boy without a sin.
Take us to that place you speak, that special place is ours to keep.

He came and went but all would find that place he said of joy and wine. All of you with hearts despair, come see what waits us there.
His pleas were heard so all would say the words he spoke to that I say. Just to listen for a change then change we'll have in exchange. For change is not a place in time, you won't find it in your mind; all can look but they won't see unless you find today in thee

Come sit with me, he asked of all of nations great and nations small. Of Abraham and Moses, he said, of Muslim faiths or Christian led.
Be not afraid of what I say if God we trust then let it lay. A place you'll find will soon appear, it's far away but oh so near.

Take it to the one who prays that life is good on any day. It matters not what others send to pull and tug at what end.

You can only see what you can touch; there is God or maybe such a time is he, not mystic tree; temptation lies beneath the sea.

He knew this in sand proclaimed; peace will come of another name. For all is truth from man or boy, the place I speak will bring you joy

Printed in the United States
33415LVS00005B/271-285

9 781413 761597